ST. JOHN CHRYSOSTOM

Eight Sermons on the Book of Genesis

ST. JOHN CHRYSOSTOM

Eight Sermons on the Book of Genesis

Translated with an Introduction
by
Robert Charles Hill

HOLY CROSS ORTHODOX PRESS
Boston, Massachusetts

ISBN 1-885652-73-9

LIBRARY OF CONGRESS CATALOGING-IN-PUBLICATION DATA

John Chrysostom, Saint, d. 407.
  [Homilies on Genesis. 1-8. English]
  Eight sermons from the Book of Genesis / translated by Robert C. Hill.
      p. cm.
  Includes bibliographical references and index.
  ISBN 1-885652-73-9 (pbk. : alk. paper)
  1. Bible. O.T. Genesis--Criticism, interpretation, etc. 2. Sermons, Greek--Translations into English. 3. Sermons, Greek--Early works to 1800. I. Hill, Robert C. (Robert Charles), 1931- II. Title.
  BR65.C43E5 2004
  222'.1106--dc22
                                    2004006079

Table of Contents

*For Everett Ferguson
in friendship and esteem*

Introduction

In the early Church, as in today's, the season of Lent prepared believers and in particular catechumens for Easter and its celebration of new life with meditation on the origin of all life; an accent on sin and repentance was also relevant. The book of Genesis (or Creation, Κτίσις, Κοσμοποιΐα, as it was also called) thus became the staple diet of Christians during those eight weeks of an Eastern Lent, and the prescribed text for preachers. John Chrysostom has left us at least three such Lenten series of sermons or homilies on Genesis from the period of his ministry as preacher in Antioch, which we can date from 386 to 389, though the second series at one point took a different turn under the influence of critical events in the city's history in that year 387, betrayed by its later name *Homilies on the Statues* (or imperial effigies, vandalized by some irate citizens).

The prior series of eight sermons (as much homiletic as the others, the English name serving only to differentiate it from the larger series of sixty-seven homilies delivered in 388 or 389) began later in Lent, if we can believe the scribal title now introducing it as ushering in Quadragesima (with its biblical overtones of forty days), or Lent's final six weeks, more familiar to us. Each evening of those weeks in that year 386 the congregation assembled (perhaps men only), at least for a sermon by the recently-ordained preacher if no Eucharist was celebrated, sometimes with other clergy in attendance and even "the father and teacher of us all," as Chrysostom refers to Bishop Flavian in the first of the series. The bishop's presence suggests the city's Great Church as the venue. Why, then, do we have only eight such sermons? We are left to wonder: sometimes a sermon is linked with the previous one by mention of "yesterday," sometimes more vaguely by "the other day," sometimes with no chronological link. Further, in this eight, unlike the longer series, the preacher does not proceed systematically through the biblical text. Again, passages in those later homilies resemble verbatim a corresponding section in the sermons (preachers, of course, are not above repeating themselves).

Transmission of the text of the Sermons

We can be confident in reading the text of the eight sermons today that we have before us the actual words delivered by Chrysostom in Antioch in that Lent of 386. Besides the assurance provided by a modern critical edition of the author's text, we can be grateful for that great resource of the early Church, the stenographers whom Eusebius amply describes in the case of Origen's homilies, and Jerome of his own staff – ταχύγραφοι, βιβλιόγραφοι, καλλί– γραφαι – who were adept at recording, editing and embellishing the words of the preacher (or dictater, in Jerome's case) for future reference. Less reliance is to be put on a criterion of Chrysostom's biographer, Dom Baur, who is pleased to find in the sermons (unlike the Genesis or Psalms homilies) evidence of spontaneity or, in his words, an "appearance of actuality," like the acknowledgement of the bishop's presence in the first sermon. We remind ourselves, however, that in a written text evidence of spontaneity can be manufactured, and we recall the celebrated instance of the speech of Cicero, another great orator in the ancient world, the *Pro Milone*, which when read later by Milo, the unsuccessful defendant enjoying his exile, prompted him to comment, "If that had been the speech given, I should not now be enjoying the mussels of Massilia (Marseille)." It is probably to the stenographers in the Great Church, however, that we owe transmission of Chrysostom's text, including the words of rebuke in Sermon Four, delivered by the disappointed preacher to a congregation that perhaps wearied of a biblical commentary that had turned into a lecture on various forms of government.

Wake up there, and dispel indifference. Why do I say this? Because
while we are discoursing to you on
the Scriptures, you instead are averting your eyes from us and fixing
them on the lamps and the man lighting the lamps. What extreme indifference is this, to ignore us and attend
to him! Here am I, lighting the fire
that comes from the Scriptures, and
the light of its teaching is burning on
our tongue. This light is brighter and
better than that light: we are not kindling a wick saturated in oil, like him:
souls bedewed with piety we set
alight with the desire for listening.

We should be sorry if the stenographer
had erased that delightful digression, en-
capsulating as it does Chryostom's high
esteem for his role of minister of the Word.

In becoming distracted that evening
when the preacher strayed from the Genesis text, the congregation was paying him
an implicit compliment for his relatively

greater skill in explicating it. In his view the biblical books are like letters sent by God and delivered by Moses, which open with the words, "In the beginning God created heaven and earth" (he says in the first sermon). Later, in the eighth sermon, the divine law on eating the fruit in the garden is like an imperial decree, which the whole amphitheatre stands in respectful silence to hear read. So he approaches the biblical text with a belief in its divine inspiration, which both Old and New Testament enjoy in speaking about Creation, if at different levels: "Do you see the relationship of both Testaments? Do you see the harmony of the teaching? Did you hear of the Creation of material things in the Old?" He is reading the book of Genesis in the local Antiochene form of the Septuagint version, which we have come to know better from the commentaries on it by Chrysostom and his fellow Antiochenes Diodore of Tarsus and Theodore of Mopsuestia (these latter two only fragmentarily extant on Genesis) and

Theodoret of Cyrus in his *Questions on the Octateuch*. In these eight sermons Chrysostom cites only a few verses from Genesis, having an agenda of his own and digressing on to questions such as the need to give alms to the poor and whether the robber on the cross was actually admitted to heaven or only to paradise, a distinction he is forced into in debate with the Manicheans. The sixty-seven homilies, by contrast, get beyond Genesis 1-3 to cover the whole book.

Interpreting Genesis

While we are disappointed, then, that the preacher did not move systematically through the first creation story in Genesis 1 or the Fall narrative in Genesis 3 (we can move to the homilies to see his treatment of each verse), what we have in the eight sermons is valuable for an insight into his hermeneutic. Though we saw him above admiring the "harmony" of the Testaments, and are somewhat taken aback at his lengthy and atypical encomium of the

Mosaic Law in the eighth sermon simply to reinforce his point (against Marcionites, it would seem) that the law in the garden about the eating of the fruit was a good thing and not responsible for the Fall, his starting point in Old Testament interpretation is that only Christian exegetes have the key to it. "While the books are from (the Jews)," he says in approaching the *crux interpretum* that is the strangely plural verb in Genesis 1:26, "the treasure of the books now belongs to us; if the text is from them, both text and meaning belong to us." Despite this superior attitude, he can be literalist and naïve in dealing with the highly figurative character of the stories of Creation and Fall: a talking serpent is taken at face value, and on the naming of animals by Adam, he simply says, "Consider how much wisdom it was with which he was filled in being able to give names to so many genera, so many different species – cattle, reptiles, birds – all properly applied. God, in fact, so far accepted the naming as never to change those names, or even remove their names when he sinned."

Unlike his fellow Antiochenes, whose commentaries on Genesis were done at their desks for studious readers who could retain the work and check its contents, Chrysostom is dealing with all comers on the spur of the moment, for whom he has to take a lowest-common-denominator approach. He therefore does not subject his LXX text to scrutiny (let alone relate it the Hebrew original, a task beyond him) by checking alternative versions, except on the rarest occasion (something he will consistently do when lecturing on the Psalms in his classroom). He does not canvass a range of predecessors' opinions on moot points of this challenging material, though he is clearly familiar with them in some cases, as in his option for "government" as the most adequate explanation of the puzzling phrase in Genesis 1:26 following that strange plural verb, "Let us make a human being *in our image*" – an explanation taken to such lengths as to encourage the distraction in Sermon Four by the lamplighter in the church. His hermeneutical option in this instance, of course, has been validated by modern linguists profiting from the results of archeology at ancient Ebla.

Validation of a less reliable kind, however, is found for the position he adopts on the respective roles of man and woman in disobedience in the garden. After ambiguously complimenting the woman on being judged a more suitable helpmate to the man than the other animals, he gives a reading of Genesis 3:16 that justifies woman's servitude and inferiority.

> I made you equal in dignity, He is saying; you abused your government: exchange it for submission. You could not bear freedom: accept slavery. You did not know how to govern, and showed this in actual practice: become one of the governed, and acknowledge your husband as your master.

This is all of a piece, he maintains, with

the thinking in 1 Timothy 2:11-14: "Listen to how Paul also speaks of this submission, so that you may learn once more the harmony of Old and New;" and he finds the key to woman's condition of subjection in this midrash of Genesis 3. Had women been present, a lamplighter would have been a welcome distraction.

Chrysostom's gifts as a preacher

Distraction during these sermons, however, was probably rare, if only because they are mostly brief by comparison with the homilies. An exception would be Sermon Seven, which (possibly in the absence of other clergy) develops into an extended debate with the Manicheans about bodily resurrection arising out of the Gospel pericope where the robber on the cross is admitted to paradise. On the other occasions, when senior clergy may have spoken, the sermon is brief, as with the eighth in the series. In either case Chrysostom's congregation generally gives every sign of being closely involved in the proceedings, even to the point of breaking out into "loud applause," if we can believe his statement of their reaction to his invitation at the close of Sermon Six to turn their home into a domestic church and ruminate on his words. There was an equally animated concurrence with his words in Sermon Four in criticism of obstreperous children, whom, in keeping with the penalty prescribed in Deuteronomy 21:18-21, they stoned (the preacher says) "with loud cries in place of stones." And they had every reason to become animated, the preacher's rhetoric being what it was: in mounting his case in Sermon Seven that human beings knew the difference between right and wrong from the outset, he cross-examines Cain about the killing of Abel more rigorously than any prosecutor.

> Why, pray, does he snatch his brother from his parents' arms and entice him out into the countryside? Why put him in an isolated area? Why deprive him of assistance? Why remove him

far from the sight of his father? Why conceal the deed if he was not aghast at his sin? Why, after committing the murder, did he quibble and lie when asked again? When God asked, remember, "Where is Abel your brother?" you replied, "Surely I am not my brother's keeper?" It is clear from this that he was clearly aware when he embarked on this deed.

Significantly, on the other hand, the digression in that same sermon on the robber in paradise, exhibiting the *makrologia* for which he became notorious, rates no mention when he summarizes the sermon in the presence of the bishop next day. The imagery the preacher employs to elicit the interest of his listeners, if conventional, is effective, drawn as it is from their experience of commerce, farming, navigation, medicine. He also shows himself to be a close observer of contemporary society: the "kindly" punishment of slaves, an institution with which he has no quarrel

(Sermon Two), execution of criminals, norms for imbibing in moderation, chastising children (Four), plight of the poor (Five), market gossip (Six). Chrysostom's congregation quickly sensed that he was in touch with the world in which they lived. We learn from the sermons, for instance, that his society had no structured approach to alleviating endemic poverty, nor did the preacher himself; he can only appeal to his congregation's generosity, guilt and fear in urging them to almsgiving to the poor assembled outside the church, as he does in closing Sermon Five with a chilling depiction of the desperation of the starving poor as night falls.

Theological accents of the Sermons
If the sermons on Genesis were delivered within a few years of the Council of Constantinople in 381 that dealt with trinitarian and Christological errors stemming from the teaching of Arius and Eunomius, these issues are not raised by the preacher (as they do obtrude into his

lectures on the Psalms to a different audience about this time). It is Creation that is in focus, at least initially; and though he does not accentuate as much as one might expect the goodness of material creation, a principal theme of Genesis 1, he wants his congregation to know that false ideas exist on this question. His panacea is simple: he offers them the opening verse, "In the beginning God made heaven and earth," as a mantra. "Even if a Manichean makes an approach, even if those with Marcion's ailment, even if those with Valentinus', even if anybody else, thrust this statement at him; even if you see him laughing, weep for him as a madman." Like Theodoret in the next generation, who sets himself the goal in his *Questions on the Octateuch* of confuting Marcionites' criticism of Old Testament statement, Chrysostom upholds the figurative account of creation of human beings in Genesis even while taking it at face value; and it is Manichean denial of bodily resurrection that prompts the lengthy digression in Sermon Seven on the admission of the robber to paradise. The unsophisticated hermeneutic applied to these chapters, however, prevents Jesus from coming frequently into focus.

Predictably, on the other hand, the focus falls often on the Fall; and the sermons provide a classically Eastern presentation of it that is full of optimism and is thoroughly Pauline, with the accent on healing rather than wound. It was out of love and concern that God punished us for the initial disobedience lest we have no sense of sin (Chrysostom says in Sermon Three). But even the punishment paled before the generous recompense. In Sermon Seven he finds confirmation in Romans 5: the Fall was a *felix culpa*.

> Hence Paul says, "Where sin abounded, grace did more abound," that is, the gift was greater than the sin; hence he also says, "The free gift is not like the fall," the human being did not sin to the extent that God gave grace, the loss was not as great as the

gain, the shipwreck was not as great as the commerce – instead, the good things outweighed the bad. And rightly so: a slave brought on the bad things, and they were less, whereas the Master granted the good things – consequently they too were greater; hence his saying, "The free gift is not like the fall."

There is not the concern for the manner in which some "original sin" was transmitted to future generations that we find in Western Fathers: all have sinned (the true sense of Romans 5:12) and so are liable, Chrysostom says in Sermon Five.

There is, in fact, a single solution to all the problems: while they were the first to sin and thus introduced slavery through disobedience on their part, once it was introduced, those who came afterwards ratified it by sins of their own. In other words, if they had been able to show that they were always free from sin, later generations would decide to object; but if they also were liable to many punishments, the basis of this claim would have no substance.

One regrets that an Augustine could not access his contemporary's thinking on this question (or properly read Paul), as well as on the impact of the Fall on human nature generally. The latter is a question on which the East again shows no negativity, though here Jesus the lamb of God enters the picture, the lamb who takes away (Chrysostom insists) not some "original sin" but "the sin of the world" (John 1:29), as is clear from the incident of the robber on Calvary, he claims: "Now, I said this lest you think you have been badly affected by the first human beings."

The root cause of the Fall, as of all our sins, he diagnoses as usual as ῥᾳθυμία, indifference, negligence, as he will conclude also in the homilies. "How is it, then," he asks the congregation in Sermon Eight, "that he fell? By his own indifference – something made clear by all who received a law and did not fall, performing instead even more than they were commanded." It is typical of Antiochene morality that sin is accountable, and conversely that reward follows human effort; the parable of the talents (a favorite locus) confirms this for the preacher in Sermon Seven. (It is a position, however, that is conveniently surrendered later in that sermon to make the point of the robber's being admitted to paradise "with a mere word, on the basis of faith alone.")

One particularly attractive feature of these sermons, especially in the conclusion of Sermon Six, is the picture the preacher paints of the domestic church, the family meditating in the privacy of their home on the word (whether the biblical word or the preacher's comment on it). It was enough, at any rate (he claims next day), to move them to enthusiastic applause.

Let us take all this to heart, then,

dearly beloved, and on returning home let us serve a double meal, one of food and the other of sacred reading; while the husband reads what has been said, let the wife learn and the children listen, and let not even servants be deprived of the chance to listen. Turn your house into a church; you are, in fact, even responsible for the salvation both of the children and of the servants. Just as we are accountable for you, so too each of you is accountable for your servant, your wife, your child.

The picture is painted in similar colors also in the tenth homily in the longer series, reminding us again of the close relationship of the two series of Lenten discourses by Chrysostom in the course of his ministry of the word in Antioch. We can envy the congregations on those occasions for the experience they enjoyed, now ourselves able to appreciate the sermons in an English translation.

Sermon One

By (581) our father Saint John Chrysostom, archbishop of Constantinople, at the beginning of the Forty Days.

On fasting, on the reason why Moses began his account with heaven and earth, and on almsgiving. [1]

Spring is welcome to mariners, spring is welcome also to farmers. But spring is not as welcome either to mariners or to farmers as the time of fasting is to people intent on having sound values, which for souls is spring of a spiritual kind, real tranquility for our reasoning. To farmers, you see, spring is welcome because it is then that they see the ground wreathed in flowers, and the growth of the plants enfolding it with a kind of mantle. To sailors spring is welcome because they can ply the ocean surface without concern, billows abated, dolphins disporting themselves in complete tranquility and often tumbling alongside the very sides of the ship. To us, on the other hand, spring is welcome because it usually represses billows, not of water in our case, but of irrational desires, and bedecks us with a wreath not of flowers but of spiritual graces. Scripture says, remember, "You will receive a wreath of graces for your head." [2] The arrival of swallows does not usually dispel winter to the extent that the coming of fasting expels the winter of our mind's passions. No longer a struggle for the soul against the flesh, nor does the handmaid rebel against the mistress; instead, all this warring of the body is at an end.

Since we enjoy deep peace, therefore, and deep tranquility as well – come now, let us also launch the vessel of instruction, dispatching it from port to the port that is the courtesy of your attentiveness. Come now, let us come to grips with more subtle ideas, exercising our minds about heaven, earth, sea and the remaining elements of creation, the text that was read to us today. What relevance to us, you ask, has the account of Creation? Well, it does have relevance to us, dearly beloved: if "the creator is perceived by analogy in the immensity and beauty of created things,"[3] we are guided to the creator to the extent that we dwell upon the beauty and immensity of created things.

It is a great good to know, on the one hand, what a created thing is and, on the other, what the creator is, what an artifact is and what the artificer: if the enemies of truth knew how to make a precise distinction between them, they would not confuse everything, putting below what is above – not that they bring stars and heaven down or elevate the earth, but that they thrust down the king of heaven from his royal throne, placed him with creation, and dignified creation with the ranking of divinity.[4] If Manicheans knew how to exercise their minds properly about creation, they would not have dignified matter that came from nothing, that is corruptible, evanescent and changeable, with the status of being unmade. If Greeks knew how to exercise their minds properly about creation, they would not have strayed from the truth, they would not have "given reverence and worship to creation instead of the creator." [5] The sky is beautiful, but the reason it was made was for you to adore its maker; the sun is brilliant, but it is for you to worship its creator. If, on the contrary, you are bent on stopping at the wonder of creation, and becoming attached to the beauty of the works, light has become darkness for you – or, rather, you have turned light (582) into darkness.

Do you see how great a good it is to know the doctrine of creation? Instead of bypassing its value, therefore, take heed precisely to what is said: we are going to speak not only of heaven, earth and sea, but also of our beginnings, whence comes death, whence a hard life, whence disappointments and worries. On these questions, you see, and on many others God composed an explanation and sent this book to us – though in fact God is not required to provide human beings with an explanation, He cries out through the prophet, "Come and let us argue it out, says the Lord." He does not only offer an explanation, however, and hold court: He even gives information on how to escape condemnation, saying not simply, "Come and let us argue it out," but first giving information on what should be said and what should be done, and then bringing to judgment. At any rate, listen to the prophetic word before this: "Wash yourselves, make yourselves clean, remove the wickedness from your souls, learn how to do good, deliver justice to the orphan and give right judgment to the widow," and then He says, "Come and let us argue it out, says the Lord."[6] I do not want to find you devoid and bereft of justification, He is saying; instead, I shall give you the advantage of an explanation and then call you to account, my wish being to have it out with you, not to condemn but to acquit. Elsewhere also He speaks this way, "Take the initiative in admitting your sins so as to be found righteous."[7] You have a harsh and unforgiving prosecutor; anticipate him by usurping his role, and shut his shameless mouth.

At the beginning, then, God communicates directly with human beings as far as it is possible for human beings to hear. This is the way He came to Adam, this the way He rebuked Cain, this the way He was entertained by Abraham. But since our nature took a turn for evil, and separated itself by a lengthy exile, as it were, at long last He sent us letters as though we were absent for a long time and He intended to reestablish the former friendship through an epistle. While it was God who sent the letters, it was Moses who brought them.[8]

Well, then, what did the letters say? *In the beginning God made heaven and earth.*[9] Why did He not speak to us about the angels, or about the archangels? After all, if the creator is discerned in created things, much more does He become visible through them. Heaven is beautiful, but not as beautiful as an angel; the sun is brilliant, but not as brilliant as an archangel; so why did He reject the higher way to lead us by the lower? Because He is speaking to Jews, with their rather irrational ways, with their attachment to material things, at that time on their way up out of Egypt where people used to worship crocodiles and dogs and apes. It was not possible to guide them to the creator by the higher way: high though that way is, it is more rugged, steep and rather direct for the weaker kind. Hence He leads them by the easier route, through heaven and earth and sea and the whole of visible creation. For proof that this is the reason, in fact, (585) listen to how the inspired author speaks to them also about the powers on high when they had made some progress: "Praise the Lord in the heavens, praise Him in the heights; praise Him, all you his angels, praise Him, all you His hosts. Because He spoke, and they were made, He commanded, and they were created." [10]

What is remarkable about this being His style of teaching in the Old Testament when even in the New, a time for instruction in higher values, Paul in speaking to the Athenians took this way which Moses had taken in instructing Jews? Even he, remember, did not speak to them of angels and archangels, but about heaven and earth and sea, preaching to them somewhat in these terms, "The God who made the world and all that is in it, as Lord of heaven and earth He does not dwell in temples made by human hand." When he spoke to the Philippians, on the other hand, he did not lead them by this way; instead, he leads them to the higher forms of creation in speaking thus, "Because by Him were created everything in heaven and on earth, whether thrones or dominions or rulers or powers – all things have been created through Him and for Him." John, too, when he had the more advanced as disciples, mentioned all creation together, saying not heaven and earth and sea, but "Everything was made through Him, and without was made not one thing that was made,"[11] visible or invisible.

Just as with teachers, you see, the teacher who receives the child from the mother teaches it the elements first, whereas the one who receives it from another teacher leads the pupil to a higher level of teaching, so too was it in the case of Moses and Paul and John: Moses came upon our nature when it was just weaned and knew nothing, and so he taught it the elements of the knowledge of God, whereas John and Paul, receiving them from master Moses, as it were, led them on to the higher level of teaching, reminding them in brief of what had preceded. Do you see the relationship of both Testaments? Do you see the harmony of the teaching? Did you hear of the creation of material things in the Old and David speaking of spiritual things, "Because He spoke, and they were created"?[12] Likewise in turn in the New, they spoke of the invisible powers, and spoke also of material creation.

In the beginning God made heaven and earth. A brief statement this, even slight, a single sentence, but capable of overthrowing the columns of the adversaries. Take an example. A Manichean comes and says, Matter is uncreated; say to him, *In the beginning God made heaven and earth*, and immediately you have overthrown all his conceit. But he does not believe the statement of Scripture, you retort. [13] On these grounds also, then, shun and avoid him as a madman: anyone who does not believe in God who has manifested Himself, and instead represents truth as falsehood – how does he not patently demonstrate his madness, his unbelief? How, he asks, could anything come from what does not exist? Tell me this on your part: how does anything come from what does exist? I mean, the fact that the earth came from what did not exist I believe, while you doubt it, whereas we both concede that a human being came from the earth. So explain what is common ground and a simpler matter, how the nature of flesh came from the earth. From earth, in fact, come mud and bricks, pottery and earthenware – but no one would ever have seen flesh coming from earth. How, then, did the nature of flesh come to be? How was bone formed? How nerves, veins and arteries? How membranes, fat, flesh, skin, nails, hair and the great variety of substances coming from the one underlying earth? You cannot explain, however; so how is it not absurd for someone professing ignorance of what is clearer and simpler to busy himself and pry into what is more difficult and more challenging?

Would you prefer that I present you with a different and simpler example, something happening each day? You will not, however, give me an explanation even of this. We eat bread every day; so how, tell me, is the very nature of bread transformed into blood, phlegm, choler and the other humors in us? After all, while it is dense and rough, blood is soft and fluid, and while the former is white or grain-colored, the latter is red and black; and if you proceed to the differences in the other qualities, you would find a great gap between bread and blood. So how does this happen, tell me, give me an explanation; but you would not be able to say. Do you then call me to account for God's creation when you are unable to provide an explanation for the change occurring in food each day? How is this not a mark of extreme folly? After all, if God is like us, call for an account for what happens – or, rather, not even in that case; after all, many things happen by human skill whose happening we cannot explain, such as how the nature of gold comes from the earth in the mines, how sand is changed into the pure substance of glass. [14] And we can cite many other instances like this, which happen by human skill, and of which we do not know the explanation. Yet even if God is like us, require an explanation; but if He is infinitely different from us and surpasses us incomparably, how would it not be a mark of utter madness to confess both His wisdom and His power as divine and incomprehensible, and yet call Him to account in the same fashion for each of the things that happen as one would some human skill?

In other words, let us abandon such reasoning and return to the unassailable rock, *In the beginning God made heaven and earth.* Rest on this foundation lest someone embroil you in the confusion of human reasoning: "The reasoning of mortals is worthless, and their designs insecure."[15] So do not forsake what is reliable by entrusting the salvation of your soul to what is unsteady and insecure; instead, stay firm in what you learned and to which you are committed, and say, *In the beginning God made heaven and earth.* Even if a Manichean makes an approach, even if those with Marcion's ailment, even if those with Valentinus', even if anybody else, thrust this statement at him; even if you see him laughing, weep for him as a madman. (585) If his countenance is ashen, his gaze lowered, and his speech restrained, don't take the bait, recognize a wolf in sheep's clothing. Abhor him for this reason in particular, that while towards you he may seem to be meek and mild as a fellow slave, towards the common Lord of all he is more savage than raging dogs, waging implacable war and battle against heaven, and bringing some force in opposition to God. Shun the venom of wickedness, hate the baleful potions, and take great care to cling to the inheritance you received from the fathers, faith and instruction from the divine Scriptures.

In the beginning God made heaven and earth. What comes first: first heaven and then earth? First the ceiling and then the floor? He is not subject to the necessity of nature, of course, nor confined to the process of workmanship: God's will is the creator and artificer of all things coming from nature and workmanship. *Now, the earth was invisible and unfinished.*[16] Why, on the one hand, did He produce heaven in an incomplete state while, on the other, Moses says He constructed earth in stages? So that you would learn His power from the superior element and thus be fully assured that He had the power to produce the latter in a finished state as He had the former. Yet for the sake of you and your salvation He did not do so. How, you ask, was it for the sake of me and my salvation? The earth is table, homeland, nourisher and mother of all alike, and city and cemetery for all alike: our bodies come from it, nourishment for our bodies come from that source, our dwelling and daily life is in it, and in due course after death we shall return to it. So lest the pressure of need bring you to marvel at it unduly, and the multiplicity of benefits put you on the slippery slope to impiety, He gives you a glimpse of it before its making as lacking form and outline so that you may see its limitations and admire the one who produces it and confers on it all its potential, the purpose being for you to glorify the one who prepares such wonderful things for your welfare.

Now, God is glorified not only through right teachings but also through a blameless life; in the words of Scripture, "Let your light shine in people's sight so that they may see your good works and glorify your Father in heaven." [17] I intended to add words about almsgiving; but it seems superfluous for me to instruct you by word when there is one seated in your midst who is capable of teaching you by deed, the father and teacher of us all. He has always made available to those hounded on all quarters for the sake of truth his ancestral home, just as if he had received it from his forebears for the very purpose of offering it for the hospitality of guests, whom he welcomes and cares for with a variety of ministrations. The result is that I am not sure if his home should be called his own or the guests' – or, rather, it should be considered his for the reason that it is the guests'. In other words, our possessions then become most of all ours when our possession of them is not for ourselves (585) but always for the poor.

How this is so, I shall explain. If you deposit your money in the poor person's right hand, no slanderer makes inroads, no envious eye sees it, no thief purloins it, no robber breaks in, no servant steals it and makes off: that safe is inviolable. If you bury it at home, on the other hand, you put the money at risk from thief, robber, envier, slanderer, servant and any harm at all. It often happens, for instance, that whereas it escapes assaults from outside, thanks to countless gates and bars, yet it does not escape the guardians, since its keepers take it and make off. Do you see that we are then masters of our possessions when we deposit them with the poor? That safer place is not only for protection, however: it is also a basis for profit and higher interest. I mean, if you lend to a human being, you get one percent, whereas if you lend to God through the poor person, you get not one percent but a hundred times a hundred percent.

And if you sow in fertile soil, when it produces a good yield, it will bear ten times what you sowed or twice as much, whereas if you sow in heaven, in addition to the hundredfold yield you will receive also eternal life, ageless and undying. Here on earth the labor is intense for those who sow, whereas there the yield appears without plow or oxen or plowmen or any other hardship, with no drought, no downpours, no blight, no hail, no army of locusts, no rivers flooding, nothing else ever to make the sowers fearful – instead, the seed sown there remains proof against all harm. So when there is no effort, no risk, no suspicion, no bad luck, and what comes up is far greater than what is sown and produces such an amount of good things "as eye has not seen, nor ear heard, nor has it entered the human heart," how would it not be a mark of extreme indifference to bypass the greater and go after the lesser, to forfeit what is secure and be involved in what is unreliable, liable to risk and a prey to constant bad luck? [18] I mean, what excuse would we have for doing this, what explanation? We constantly plead poverty; but we are not poorer than that famous widow who had only two mites and contributed them. [19]

So let us emulate this woman's wealth, let us imitate the magnanimity of her goodwill, so as to attain also the good things laid up for her. May it be the good fortune of us all to be granted this, thanks to the prayers and intercession of the priests and the grace of lovingkindness of our Lord Jesus Christ, to whom with the Father and the Holy Spirit be glory, power and honor, now and forever, for ages of ages. Amen.

Sermon Two

In the same text, why in the case of sun,
moon, sky and the other things
he said, Let it be, *but in the case*
of the human being Let us make.

And what the phrase in the image *means.*

Surely you remember the questions raised with you the other day?[1] You prompted us to such a degree of presumption and temerity as even at that stage to touch on the questions. Or, rather, it was not a matter even of temerity and presumption: far from relying on our own resources, we (587) entrusted everything to the clergy's prayers and yours, and girded ourselves for the contest. The Church's prayer is so efficacious that even if we were less vocal than stones, it would render our tongue lighter than any feather; after all, just as a breeze blowing directly into a ship's sails propels the vessel more swiftly than an arrow, so the Church's prayer blows upon the speaker's tongue and propels his words more powerfully than a breeze.[2]

Hence we, too, are confident in each day girding ourselves: if in the case of worldly contests anyone with only ten or twenty supporters in the crowd descends into the arena with enthusiasm, much more shall we, when not only ten or twenty but the whole stadium is drawn from our brethren and fathers, have confidence in doing so. Admittedly, in the case of worldly contests the contestant gains nothing from the spectator except his shouting, commending the achievements and giving opposition to the adversaries while seated above; it is not permissible to go down into the arena, lend a hand, pull the adversary's feet or make any such demonstration. In fact, the organizers of those contests from the outset fix sharp stakes and wreath them in ropes to contain the spectators' frenzy. And what is remarkable about a spectator's not being permitted to go down into the arena when they seat even the trainer outside in the dust and bid him offer the contestants instructions from a distance, but do not allow him to come near? Here, on the contrary, it is not like that; instead, it is possible both for instructor and for spectator to come down, to be close in spirit and combine forces in our prayers.

So come now, let us begin our task in the manner of those very athletes: when they lay hold of one another out in the middle, by the force of the hold they are thrust towards the crowd surrounding them outside on account of the size of the ring, and loosing their hold they resume the position of contest again. On resuming, however, they do not engage in upright stance this time, but put themselves in the same grip as they were in when they broke. In our case, then, since it was not limitations of space but of time that forced us to interrupt the sermon, come now, let us return to the place of the contest and loose the grip that held us yesterday. *God said*, remember, *Let us make the human being in our image and likeness.* [3] One question is worth asking first: why on earth is it that, when heaven is made, the expression is not *Let us make* but *Let there be heaven, Let there be light*, and so on with each part of creation, whereas here the term *Let us make* alone occurs, counsel and consideration and reference to someone else of equal standing? Who is it, then, who is about to be created, the object of such wonderful esteem? It is a human being, the great and marvelous animal, more precious to God than all creation, on whose account exist earth and heaven and sea and all the rest of creation – a human being, whose salvation God so loved as not to spare even the Only-begotten on their account. [4] He did not desist, in fact, from doing and devising everything until He led them up and (588) seated them at His right hand. Paul even cries aloud, "With Him He has raised us up and seated us at His right hand in the heavenly places through Christ Jesus."[5] Hence counsel and consideration and reference, not that God needs counsel – perish the thought – but that by the expression of the words He shows us the esteem for the one made.

If more estimable than the whole world, you ask, how is it that they are produced after the world? For the very reason that they are more estimable than the world: just as when an emperor is due to process into some city, generals and lieutenants and bodyguards and all the slaves precede him so as to prepare the palace, have every convenience prepared and welcome the emperor with great honor, just so too here, with an emperor about to be brought forth, as it were, the sun preceded, the moon went ahead, the light entered, everything was made and got ready, and only then the human being is brought forth at a later stage with great honor.

Let us make a human being in our image. Let the Jew give heed: to whom does God say, *Let us make*? The text is from Moses, from Moses in whom they claim to believe, though in fact they lie. For proof that they lie and do not believe, listen to Christ talking to them and saying, "If you believed Moses, you would believe in me."[6] Now, while the books are from them, the treasure of the books now belongs to us; if the text is from them, both text and meaning belong to us. So to whom did He say, *Let us make a human being*? He merely addresses an angel, you say, or an archangel: just as knaves called to account by their masters, lacking the ability to give a direct reply, blurt out anything that enters their heads, so too do you behave, claiming, He spoke to an angel or an archangel. What kind of angel? What kind of archangel? After all, creating does not belong to angels, or doing these deeds to archangels. Why was it that in making heaven He did not speak to angel and archangel but produced it of Himself, whereas in producing the being more estimable than heaven and the whole world

– namely, the human being – He then gives all the servants a share in its creation?

This is not how it happened, this is not the way: it belongs to angels to be in attendance, not to create, to archangels to serve, not to share in decision and counsel. Listen to what Isaiah says of the seraphim powers, who are superior to the archangels: "I saw the Lord seated on the throne lofty and exalted, and the seraphim in attendance around Him, each with six wings; with two wings they covered their faces" (obviously protecting their eyes on account of their inability to bear the brilliance emitted from the throne).[7] What are you saying – the seraphim were in attendance, struck by this wonder despite experiencing God's considerateness,[8] while angels share His decision and participate in His deliberation? That makes no sense, however. Well, who is it to whom He says, *Let us make* (589) *a human being*? Wonderful counselor, figure of authority, mighty God, prince of peace, father of the world to come, God's only-begotten Son in person. [9] It is to Him that He says, *Let us make a human being in our image and likeness* — not "my" and "your" image but *ours*, [10] indicating one image and one likeness. Now, God and angels do not have the one image and the one likeness: how could there be one image and likeness of master and servants?

And so on all grounds your claim is disqualified; here, in fact, His reference is to image in the sense of government, as the sequel indicates: after saying, *in our image and likeness*, He went on, *and let them govern the fish of the sea.* God's government, however, and angels' would not be one and the same: how could it be, slaves' and master's, servants' and bidder's? Some other people in turn, nevertheless, persist in making the claim to us that God has the same kind of image as we do, taking the term in an improper sense; He did not mean image of being but image of government, as we shall make clear from the sequel. [11] For proof, in fact, that the divinity does not have human form listen to Paul's words, "A man ought not wear a veil, since he is God's image and glory, whereas a woman, being a man's glory, ought to wear a veil on her head." Actually he used "image" here to refer to the lack of difference in form with respect to God, and the human being is called "image of God" for the reason that God is also configured this way. In their view, therefore, not only the man should be called *image* but also the woman, since woman and man have one outline, stamp and likeness.

Why, then, is the man referred to as God's image, but no longer the woman? Because he is not using *image* in terms of form, but *image* in respect of government, which the man alone has, but no longer the woman as well. After all, he is subject to no one, whereas she is under him, as God said, "Your turning will be towards your husband, and he will lord it over you." [12] Hence the man is the image of God, since he has no one over him, just as there is no one above God, who governs everything; the woman, on the other hand, is the man's glory, since she is subject to the man. At another time he says elsewhere, "We must not think the divinity is like gold, silver stone, artistic representation or human desire." [13] Now, his meaning is something like this: the divinity not only transcends visible figures, but the mind would not be able to make an adequate design of God. So how could God have the form of a human being when Paul says that no mind is capable of even making a figure of God's being? We would all, in fact, by ourselves simply make a representation of our own shape and outline in keeping with our ideas.

Once again my intention was this time as well to append a discourse on almsgiving, but the occasion does not allow us. Hence we shall leave it unsaid for the time, giving you this recommendation, to hold fast to all that was said and make an upright life your deep concern so that we may not (890) have assembled idly and to no purpose. After all, even if we maintain correctness in doctrine without attending to the practice of virtue, we shall miss out completely on eternal life; Scripture says, remember, "It is not the one who says, Lord, Lord, who will enter the kingdom of heaven, but the one who does the will of my Father, who is in heaven." [14] Let us therefore do God's will in all zeal, loyalty and enthusiasm so as to be in a position to enter heaven and gain the good things laid up for those who love God. May it be the good fortune of us all to attain this, thanks to the grace of Christ, to whom with the Father and Holy Spirit be glory, honor and power, for ages of ages. Amen.

Sermon Three

In the same text, what is the meaning of the phrase in our likeness, *why is it that though God told us to govern the wild animals, we do not, and that it arises from deep solicitude.*

Just as the sowers gain no benefit when the seed is thrown along the road, likewise there will be no advantage even for the speaker if the discourse does not reach the mind of the listeners, and instead his voice is toneless, is simply scattered to the winds and leaves the listener clueless. Now, far from having no point in saying this, my purpose is to prevent your being merely bewildered by the simpler ideas, and instead for you to make an effort to plumb even the more profound ones. After all, if we were not at this point to descend to the depths of the Scriptures when our limbs are light enough for swimming, our eye is all the sharper for no longer being clouded with the evil flow of indulgence, and our spirit is more ready to resist being stifled, when would we descend? When there is indulgence, banqueting, imbibing and a table groaning to excess? No, that is not the time for us to be easily moved, when the heavy burden of indulgence weighs down the spirit. Do you not see that even people wanting to find precious stones do not find what they are after by sitting on the beach above the surface counting the waves? Instead, they dive to the very depths, though great effort is involved in the search, considerable risk in the discovery and little gain after the discovery. I mean, what great contribution does the discovery of precious stones make to our life? Would that it did not introduce great evils: nothing so overwhelms our life and turns everything upside down as a frenzy for possessions. [1]

While people like that, however, still risk body and soul for daily sustenance and brave the waves, here by contrast there is no risk, the effort is not so extreme – instead, it is rare and light for the added reason of retaining what is found; people generally think that what is easily found is of no great value. In the ocean of the Scriptures there is no buffeting from waves: this ocean is calmer than any harbor, there is no need to descend into the gloomy caverns of the deep, nor commit the safety of one's person to the rush of irrational waters. Instead, here there is a strong light brighter than the sun's rays, there is deep peace, no tempest in the offing, the value of what is found so great as to defy description. Instead of being lethargic, then, let us take to the search. You heard that God made the human being in the image of God, and we explained the meaning of the phrase *in image and likeness*, namely, not a similarity of being but a likeness by way of government, and that *in likeness* means being mild and gentle, and as far as possible being like God on the basis of virtue, as Christ says, "Be like my Father, who is in heaven."[2]

In other words, just as in this wide and spacious land some animals are more irrational and some more savage, likewise in the reaches of our soul some thoughts are more irrational and beastly, others wilder and more savage. There is therefore need to take charge and get the better of them, and to entrust government of them to reasoned thinking. And how, you ask, would one get the better of untamed thinking? What are you saying, human being that you are? We get the better of lions and tame their spirits, and you are uncertain of being able to transform untamed thinking to mildness? Admittedly, to a lion wildness is natural, mildness unnatural, whereas to you it is the opposite, gentleness being natural and savagery unnatural. Will the person who drives out of the wild animal what is natural and instills what is unnatural fail to preserve what is natural in their own soul? What awful indifference would that not exemplify? In the case of the lions' soul there is the further difficulty that an animal's soul is devoid of reason – though you have often seen lions tamer than sheep being led through the marketplace, and many people in the shops are in the habit of throwing money to the owner as a reward for his skill and cleverness in taming the animal. In the case of your soul, on the other hand, there is reason, fear of God and much assistance from all quarters. So cite me not pretexts and excuses: it is possible for you to be meek and mild if you want to.

Let us make a human being in our image and likeness; and let them govern the wild animals. At this point Greeks will spring at us and claim the verse defies the truth: we do not govern the wild beasts – they govern us and cause us deep apprehension. To begin with, this is not quite true: a human being has only to appear to cause an animal to make off, such being the fear they have of us. On the other hand, if in some cases they attack to defend themselves, either under pressure of hunger or often when we corner them or bring them to a point of desperation, it does not follow that this is the result of imperfect government. After all, if on seeing brigands invading, you were to arm yourself and proceed to defend yourself, it would not be a question of government but (592) deep concern for your own welfare.

I am not making my case on this basis, however, but on another, which it would also be useful for you to hear. We fear and dread the wild animals, and fall short of governing them; far from denying this, I personally admit it. This does not prove God's law is false, however: in the beginning this was not the case, the animals being in fear and trembling, and submitting to the human being as master. But since we lost their confidence and respect, we accordingly dread them. Proof of this? *God brought the animals to Adam to see what he would call them.* Instead of taking to his heels as though in fear, Adam gave them all names as though submissive slaves, which is a sign of lordship. Hence, in His wish to show him through this the high level of His authority as well, He entrusted him with the imposition of names, and the ones given by him remained current: *They all had the name Adam gave them.*[3] This, of course, is one sign that in the beginning the wild beasts were not frightening to the human being, and the second is even clearer, the serpent's conversation with the woman. I mean, if the animals were frightening to human beings, the woman would not have held her ground on seeing the serpent, but would have taken off; she would not have accepted his advice, she would not have talked with it with such ease, but would immediately have been astonished at the sight and made off. As it was, however, she entered into discussion and was not afraid, there being no such fear at that stage. But when sin came on the scene, the basis of respect also disappeared; and just as with servants, while the upright ones are objects of respect to their fellow servants, whereas those who have given offense are afraid even of their fellows, so too is it with the human beings. You see, as long as they enjoyed familiarity with God, they were frightening to the animals; but after they offended, they were then afraid even of the least of their fellow slaves. Now, if this is not so, show me on your part that the animals were frightening to the human beings – but you would not be able.

If, on the other hand, fear should come on the scene after this event, it too is a sign of God's solicitude. You see, if the dignity given the human beings by God had remained unaffected when the commandment given them by Him was overturned and set aside, they would not easily have risen; after all, when both obedient and disobedient people enjoy the same dignity, they are schooled rather in wickedness and do not readily desist from vice. I mean, if as it is they cannot bear to contain themselves when fear and punishments and sanctions are in force, what would they be like if they felt no consequences of the crimes they committed? So it is clear that it was out of care and concern for us that God deprived us of government.[4]

Consider in this as well, I ask you, His ineffable lovingkindness: Adam completely violated the commandment and broke the law, whereas instead of completely abolishing his dignity and completely stripping him of authority, God exempted from his government only those animals that did not make a great contribution to his livelihood, leaving under his control those that were necessary, useful and able to be a great service to our way of life. He left herds of oxen for us to plough the field, to till the soil, to sow the seed; (593) He left the species of beasts of burden to share our labor in transporting loads; He left flocks of sheep for us to have an adequate supply of garments to wear, and He made provision for other species of animals to meet many other of our needs. Since in punishing the human being, remember, He had said, *In the sweat of your face you shall eat your bread,*[5] in case this sweat and toil and labor should be unbearable, He lightened the pressure and burden of the sweat with the great number of the brute beasts called into service with us in this labor and hardship. And just as a loving and caring master, after scourging his servant, applies some ointment to the wounds, so too God, in carrying out a sentence, wishes in every way to make this sentence lighter, on the one hand sentencing us to constant sweat and hardship, and on the other arranging for many species of brute beasts to be pressed into service with us in the hard work.

Let us give thanks to Him for all this: if you examine it, His gift of dignity, subsequent removal of the dignity, not removing all the dignity, instilling in us fear of the wild animals, and everything else is characterized by great wisdom, deep concern, much lovingkindness. May it be the good fortune of us all to enjoy this constantly to the glory of God, who is responsible for it; to Him be the glory for ages of ages. Amen.

Sermon Four

In the same text, the fact that sin introduced three forms of slavery,

and in reference to indifferent listeners and those who do not honor their parents.

Yesterday you heard how God made the human being king and governor of the wild animals, and how He immediately stripped them of kingship – or, rather, not God but they stripped themselves of this dignity through disobedience.[1] Attaining kingship, you see, was the result of God's lovingkindness alone; in fact, it was not as a reward for good behavior that He gave it to them, adorning them with the dignity before they were made. In other words, to prevent your claiming that the human beings were made later, then performed many good deeds and thus won God over to giving them government of the animals, on the point of forming them God speaks about their government in these terms, *Let us make a human being in our image and likeness, and let them govern the animals of the earth.* The dignity is conferred before life, the crown before creation; even before being made they are conducted to the royal throne. You see, while human beings confer honor on their subjects in extreme old age after many hardships and countless dangers, some in peace and some in war, God is not like that: as soon as they were made, He installed them in this position of honor so as to bring out that what was conferred was not a reward for good behavior, but on God's part was gratuitous, not due to them. While their receiving government was the result of God's lovingkindness alone, then, their forfeiting government was the result of their indifference:[2] just as kings discharge from government those who disobey their commands, so too did God in the case of human beings, discharging them from government at that time.

Now, it is necessary to explain today the great honor of another kind as well, which sin of its nature removed, and all the forms of slavery it introduced, like a kind of usurper with a variety of shackles shackling our nature in its various roles of government. First, then, is the form of government and of slavery by which men have power also over women, there being need of this after sin. Before the disobedience, you see, she was equal in dignity to the man: when God formed her; the words He had used in the formation of the man he used also in the creation of the woman. As He had said in his case, then, *Let us make a human being in our image and likeness*, and did not say, Let there be a human being, likewise in her case as well He did not say, Let there be a woman, but here too *Let us make him a helpmate*, and not simply *a helpmate* but *like him*, again indicating her equality of dignity. Since, you see, the brute beasts made a helpful contribution to our needs in life, lest you should think the woman also is one of the slaves, notice how He makes the difference obvious: *He paraded the animals before Adam, and no helpmate like him was found for him.*[3] What does that mean – that the horse, that goes to battle with him, is not a helpmate? That the ox, that pulls the plow and labors with him in sowing the seed, is not a helpmate? That the ass and the mule, that work with him in transporting his burdens, are not helpmates? Lest you say so, He accordingly makes a precise distinction: He did not say simply, No helpmate was found for him, but *No helpmate like him was found for him.* Likewise here, too, He did not say simply, Let us make him a helpmate, but *Let us make him a helpmate like him.*[4]

Now, this was before sin; but after sin *For your husband will be your yearning, and he will be your master.* I made you equal in dignity, He is saying; you abused your government: exchange it for submission. You could not bear freedom: accept slavery. You did not know how to govern, and showed this in actual practice: be-

come one of the governed, and acknowledge your husband as your master. *For
your husband will be your yearning, and he
will be your master.*[5] See God's lovingkindness in this, too: lest on hearing *You will
be his master* you think his being lord is
burdensome, He put the term denoting
care first, *For your husband will be your
yearning*, that is to say, Your refuge, ha-
ven and security is what he will be for you;
in all the troubles that develop it is he that
I allow you to yearn for and take refuge
in. And not only in that regard: He also
bound them together by natural necessity,
encircling them in a chain of desire like
some unbreakable bond.

Do you see how, while sin introduced
submission, God in His design and wisdom also employed these to our advantage? Listen to how Paul also speaks of
this submission so that you may learn
once more the harmony of Old and New:
"Let a woman learn in silence with full
submission." Do you see Him, too, subjecting the woman to the man? But wait a

while, and listen to the actual reason: why does He say "with full submission"? "I do not allow a woman to teach." Why? Once she taught Adam wrongly. "Nor to have authority over a man." Why not? (595) Once she used authority wrongly. "Only to keep silence." Give the reason for that, too. "It was not Adam who was deceived: the woman was deceived, and became a transgressor." Hence He forced her down from the throne of teaching. In other words, He is saying, let the one who does not know how to teach learn; but if they refuse to learn and still want to teach, they will be the ruination of both themselves and the pupils – which is what happened at that time in the woman's case. [6]

While the fact that she has been subjected to the man, however, and that it was through sin that she was subjected, is clear from this, what I want to hear is the verse *For your husband will be your yearning, and he will be your master*. I want to find out how Paul speaks of this solicitude and combines lordship with affection. Where, then, does he do it? In writing to the Corinthians he says, "Husbands, love your wives" – see the verse *For your husband will be your yearning* – "Wives should respect their husbands" [7] – see the verse *He will be your master.* Do you see how trouble-free the lordship when the lord is an ardent lover of the subject, when fear is accompanied by love? In this way, in fact, the burdensome element of subjection is removed. Disobedience, then, ushered in one form of government; have regard, not to the fact that God schooled her in her duty, but to the fact that sin was responsible for servitude in reality.

There is also a second kind of servitude, which is more burdensome than the first and which takes its beginning and origin from sin. After the deluge in the time of Noah, remember, the flood over the whole world and the utter devastation, Ham sinned against his father, even by looking on him in his nakedness, and he aggravated his nakedness by leveling an accusation against him to his brothers, and thus became the servant of his brothers; the malice of his will undermined his natural nobility, and rightly so. Scripture, you see, pieces together countless excuses for the righteous man – or, rather, it provides him with a complete acquittal in one word, "Noah was the first farmer," the word "first" containing adequate defense for his drunkenness: he was aware neither of the quantity of wine he should drink nor of the way to drink it, whether plain or mixed with water, nor when to drink, whether immediately on drawing it from the vat or after waiting a while.[8] So while Scripture excuses Noah on these grounds, his offspring on the contrary, who was saved by him (it was owing to his father's reputation, remember, that he did not perish in the flood along with the rest), who had no regard for nature itself and no recollection of his survival, who was not brought to his senses by fear, who still had before his eyes the abiding effects of God's wrath and the visible traces of the disaster, and who felt the fear arising from what had happened, ridiculed his parent. This is the reason a certain sage also offers this exhortation, "Take no satisfaction in your father's disgrace: your father's disgrace is no credit to you."[9] Not even this, however, did the fellow acknowledge; he committed a sin too grave for any pardon or excuse. Hence he incurred servitude as a penalty for the sin, became his brothers' servant, and through the malice of his will he forfeited the prerogative of nature.

See also a second form of slavery: do you want to find out about a third as well, more burdensome than the previous two and much more frightening? Since, in fact, they did not bring us to our senses, God multiplied the bonds. What is this form, then? That of rulers, that of officials, not like the one the woman had, not like the one slaves have, but far more frightening. Everywhere, you see, one can spy sharpened swords, executioners, penalties, torture, punishments, the power of life and death. For proof that this form of government necessarily followed from sin, listen

in turn to Paul himself giving the rationale for it: "If you want to have no fear of
authority, do the right thing, and you will
win its commendation. But if you do the
wrong thing, have fear: the sword is not
carried to no purpose." [10] Do you see that
ruler and sword are there for wrongdo-
ers? In any case, listen to a still clearer
statement of this: "It brings vengeance to
the wrongdoer." He did not say, A ruler is
not without purpose: what, then? "The
sword is not carried to no purpose." He
appointed you an armed judge: just as a
loving father in his goodness entrusts to
fearsome tutors and teachers children
who ignore him and scorn his fatherly affection, so too God in His goodness entrusted to rulers, like teachers and tutors,
our nature that scorned Him, the purpose
being for them to correct their neglect.

If you would prefer, however, let us see
the same point being made also in the Old
Testament, that it was on account of sin
that there was need for this form of government as well. Provoked by wrongdo-

ers, one of the prophets puts it somehow like this, "Will you keep silent when the impious devour the righteous, and will you treat people like the fish of the sea and reptiles, without a leader?" [11] This, then, is the purpose of a leader, to stop our being like reptiles, this the purpose of a ruler, to prevent out devouring one another like fish: just as medicines are the result of ailments, so punishments are the result of sins. At any rate, for proof that the person living a life of virtue does not need supervising on that account, listen to what Paul says, "If you want to have no fear of authority, do the right thing, and you will win its commendation." The judge is your overseer, he is saying: if you live a law-abiding life, he will not only oversee but also commend you. And what am I to say of the need for rulers when those pursuing sound values are superior to other important people? The laws, in fact, are rulers for rulers, but the person living a simple life has no need even of laws; hear what Paul says on this, "A law is not there for the righteous." [12] And if a law is not there, much less has a ruler been appointed. Here, then, is the third form of government, which also has its basis in sin and wickedness. (597)

So what does Paul mean, "Authority comes only from God"? [13] He established it for our benefit: while sin created the need for it, God used it to our advantage. Just as the need for medicine comes from ailments, and the administering of the medicine depends on the physicians' skill, so too the need for servitude came from sin, and its proper control depends on God's wisdom.

Wake up there, and dispel indifference. Why do I say this? Because while we are discoursing to you on the Scriptures, you instead are averting your eyes from us and fixing them on the lamps and the man lighting the lamps. [14] What extreme indifference is this, to ignore us and attend to him! Here am I, lighting the fire that comes from the Scriptures, and the light of its teaching is burning on our tongue. This light is brighter and better than that light: we are not kindling a wick saturated in oil, like him: souls bedewed with piety we set alight with the desire for listening. Paul, too, at one time was speaking in an upper room – not that anyone should think I am comparing myself to Paul (I am not so mad): it is rather for you to learn the great degree of interest you should take in listening – Paul, then, was speaking in an upper room, evening was falling as it is now, and in the upper room there were lamps. Then Eutyches fell from the window without the fall interrupting the assembly or the fatality breaking up the spectacle; instead, they were so rapt in attending to the divine sayings that no one noticed the fall. [15] You, by contrast, see nothing strange or unusual – only someone doing a routine task – and you switch your eyes in that direction. What excuse would that deserve? Let no one, therefore, dearly beloved, think the rebuke in any way harsh: it is not out of dislike but solicitude that we correct you. Scripture says, remember, "Wounds from friends are more worthy of trust than the spontaneous kisses of enemies." [16]

So wake up, I beg you, ignore this fire and pay attention to the fire of the divine Scriptures. It is, in fact, a different form of government I wish to mention to you, taking its origins not in sin but from nature itself. So what it is, then? That of parents towards their offspring: such respect is a reward for birth pangs. Hence someone has said, "Serve like masters those who bore you;" he then goes on to give the reason as well: "After all, how can you repay them for what they did for you?" [17] In fact, is there any way at all that a child can repay his father? So he means nothing other than this: you will not be able to give birth to them as they gave birth to you. Since we fail by comparison in this, then, in another respect let us be prodigal in the honor we give them, not only because of the law of nature but out of fear of God prior to the law. God, you see, is very anxious for parents to be honored by those they bore, rewarding with great benefits and gifts those who do so, and punishing with severe and dire calamities those who transgress the law. "Let the one who maligns father or mother be put to death," Scripture says. (598) To those who honor them, on the other hand, He speaks in terms like this, "Honor your father and your mother so that it may be well for you, and you may live long on the earth." [18] What is thought the highest good, a ripe old age and length of life, He awarded as a prize to those honoring them; and what seems to be the ultimate calamity, untimely death, He assigned as a punishment to those maltreating them, winning over the former to benevolence with the promise of esteem, and dissuading the latter from maltreatment through fear of punishment, even against their will.

He does not simply gives orders for the death of the parricide, in fact, nor for executioners to take him from the court and lead him out through the marketplace, or even behead him outside the city: the father personally parades him before the city, and is given credit without any proof – and rightly so. After all, the one who had chosen to spend on his child money, personal attention and everything else would never turn accuser unless there were an extraordinary degree of maltreatment. He therefore parades him before the city, then summons the whole population and delivers the accusation; all the listeners one by one take up a stone and then hurl it at the parricide. [19] The lawgiver, you see, wants them not only to be witnesses of the punishment but also to implement it, so that each of them on seeing their own right hand, by which they personally cast a stone at the parricide, may have sufficient prompting to good behavior. Now, the lawgiver suggests to us not only this, but as well the point that those who maltreat their parents do wrong not only to them but also to everyone. Hence His calling everyone to take part in the punishment, as though everyone was maltreated, and He has the populace and the whole city gather round, His purpose being to teach the lesson that, though having no common bond with those wronged, they are so indignant at the maltreatment of parents that for the maltreatment of their common humanity they will drive such a person, like some plague and common disease, not only from the city but even from life itself. Such a person, in fact, is also common enemy to everyone – to God, to human nature, to the laws, to the life common to us all; hence He bids every-one be involved in the execution as though performing a cleansing of the city.

May many good things come your way for so gladly accepting the discourse on the parricide, and stoning him with loud cries in place of stones: [20] it is a sign that each of you shows great benevolence for your own father. Normally, in fact, we have particular admiration for the laws that punish sins when we are not con-scious of sins in our own case. For all this let us give thanks to the loving God who cares for our life, who looks after parents and is concerned for children, and who arranges everything for our welfare. To Him belongs glory, honor and adoration together with the Father, who is without beginning, and to the Holy Spirit, now and forever, for ages of ages. Amen. (599)

Sermon Five

*In the same text, that we are not punished
on Adam's account,*

*that the benefits accruing through him are
greater than the troubles,*

and against those who bypass the poor.

It is perhaps your opinion that our treatment of lordship was complete; my view, on the other hand, is that much fruit is still appearing in it. Do not tire, I ask you, until we have harvested it all. When hardworking farmers see a vine covered in foliage and weighed down with fruit, remember, they do not only cut the outside clusters, but also go further in, bending back the branches and pushing down the foliage to prevent even the smallest parts of a bunch being hidden by the leaves and escaping notice. So do not prove to be more indifferent than they, or give up until you have taken everything, especially since, though the labor is mine, the yield is yours. [1]

Yesterday we leveled an accusation at women – or, rather, not women, only Eve – for introducing servitude through sin. [2] Women would reply to us, Why are we condemned for her sin, and one person's fall became a charge against all humankind? Slaves also would say, Why on earth was it that, when Ham was insolent to his father, the effects of sin were transmitted to the whole race? People in fear of governors would also make a complaint as to why it is that, when others were living a life of wickedness, they were the ones consigned to the yoke of government. So what reply would we give to all these people? There is, in fact, a single solution to all the problems: while they were the first to sin and thus introduced slavery through disobedience on their part, once it was introduced, those who came afterwards ratified it by sins of their own. In other words, if they had been able to show that they were always free from sin, later generations would decide to object; but if they were even liable to many punishments, the basis of this claim would have no substance.[3] My statement, in fact, was not that sin does not henceforth introduce sin; it was that every sin has been associated with slavery, and my censure was directed at the nature of sin, not at a solitary kind of sin. Just as all incurable diseases bring one to the point of death without all being of the same nature, therefore, so too all sins give rise to slavery without all being of the same nature. Eve sinned by tasting of the tree, and was condemned for it; accordingly, in your turn do not commit a sin that is different but perhaps graver than hers. It is worth saying this both in the case of slaves and in the case of the governed, that while the first parents introduced sin, their successors clung to the power of lordship by the sins they committed.

I can supply the rationale for this in

other ways as well – for example, many people were freed from lordship by returning to virtue. First, let us launch our case by citing the case of women for you to see how blessed Paul, who put shackles on them, was also the one in turn to undo them. "If a woman has an unbeliever for her husband, (600) and he consents to live with her, she is not to dismiss him." Why? "For all you know, you might save your husband."[4] How, you ask, can a wife save him? By teaching, instructing, encouraging to a consideration of piety. Yesterday, to be sure, blessed Paul, you said, "I allow no woman to teach;" so how is it you go on to make her the teacher of her husband? Far from contradicting myself, I am actually quite consistent. At any rate, listen to why he disqualified her, and why in turn he promotes her to the position of teaching, so that you may discover Paul's wisdom. Let a man teach, he says. Why? Because he was not deceived; the text says, "Because Adam was not deceived." Let a woman learn, he says. Why? Because she was deceived; the text says, "The woman was deceived and became a transgressor."[5] In the present case, on the other hand, the opposite is true: since the husband is a non-believer and the wife a believer, let the wife do the teaching, he says. Why? Because she has not been deceived, being a believer. So let the husband do the learning: he was deceived, being a non-believer. The role of teaching has been reversed, he is saying; now let the exercise of lordship also be reversed. Do you see in each case he shows lordship following upon deceit and sin, not upon nature? From the beginning, then, deceit came to the woman, and subjection followed upon deceit; later deceit was transferred to the man, and subjection was also transferred. And just as in the beginning he entrusted the salvation of the woman to the man, since he was not deceived, the text saying, "For your husband shall your yearning be, and he will be your master,"[6] so here as well in the case of the believer with the non-believer as a husband he entrusts the salvation of the husband to the wife in the words, "For all you know, you may save your husband." What proof could be clearer than this that slavery follows upon sin, not upon nature?

This is applicable also to slaves: "Were you a slave when called? Do not be concerned about it." Do you see how once again the title "slave" is of no consequence when virtue is present? "But even if you cannot gain your freedom, make better use of it," that is, instead remain as a slave." Why? "For whoever was called in the Lord as a slave is a freed person belonging to the Lord."[7] Do you see how his slavery was in name only, whereas in reality he enjoyed freedom? But why did He let him continue as a slave? For you to learn the bounty of freedom: just as keeping the bodies of the three boys unharmed with the furnace still burning was much more remarkable than extinguishing it,[8] so demonstrating His freedom with slavery in force was much more important and more remarkable than freeing him from it. Hence He says, "Even if you cannot gain your freedom, make better use of it," that is, remain a slave: you enjoy freedom in the truest sense.

Do you want to see this point illustrated also in the case of the governed? Nebuchadnezzar was a king who lit a furnace with great ferocity and paraded the three boys, who were young, isolated, with no one to protect them, slaves, captives, people without a country. He asked, "Is it true, Shadrach, Meshach and Abednego, that you do not worship my gods, and (601) do not bow down to the golden statue that I set up?" So what of them? Observe how virtue made these captives more kingly than the king, and brought out their more elevated attitude. As though not speaking to a king, in fact, but dealing with a subject, they replied forthrightly in these terms, "We have no need to give a reply to the king in this matter," that is, we shall give a demonstration not in words but in actions. "God in heaven is able to save us." [9] They reminded him of the favor given to Daniel, using the same words as the prophet had used at that time. What was it he said? "The explanation the king requires comes not from soothsayers, astrologers and magicians; instead, it is the God in heaven who reveals mysteries." [10] So they remind him of this statement so as to render him more amenable. They then said, "If not, let it be known to you, O King, that we do not worship your gods, and do not bow down to the golden statue you set up." [11] Observe those young men's wisdom: in case those present at that time should accuse God of weakness if they happened to be cast into the furnace and die, they took the initiative in confessing His power in the words, "It is God in heaven who is able to save us." And in case they should succeed in escaping the flames, and be thought to serve God by way of recompense, they went on, "If not, let it be known to you, O King, that we do not worship your gods, and do not bow down to the golden statue you set up." They thus at the one time proclaimed God's power and demonstrated their soul's fortitude lest someone say of them as well what the devil said of Job by way of calumny. What did the devil say of Job? "It is not without reward that Job reverences you: you put a fence around his goods inside and out."[12] Lest anyone be in a position to say this of them, therefore, they took the initiative in stopping their shameless mouth.

As I said, however, even if a person is a captive, a slave, a stranger, living in a foreign land, and is faithful to the practice of virtue, they will be more kingly than kings. Do you see the release from slavery in the case of women, of servants, of the governed?

Come now, I shall at this point show you also the expulsion of fear of wild animals. At one time in the same city of Babylon they threw Daniel into a pit, but the lions did not dare touch him: [13] they saw in him the ancient and regal image in all its splendor, they gazed upon that imprint which they saw in the case of Adam before sin, approaching Adam with the same submissiveness and receiving their names at that time. This happened not only here, but also in the case of blessed Paul: he landed on the island of savages and sat down by the fire to warm himself; a viper then emerged from the firewood and fastened on his hand. So what happened then? The animal immediately fell off: not finding sin, it could not bite; instead, just as in our case, when we want to clamber up some smooth promontory and find nothing to hold on to, we immediately fall down, whether it be sea or sheer drop beneath, so too the animal, despite a fire burning beneath it, did not find sin to hang on to or any place to sink its fangs, fell down into the fire and perished. [14]

Do you want me to give you also a third rationale? The first was this, that not only our first parents but also those coming after them have sinned; the second, that the virtuous, even while living in the present life, experience a lighter slavery –

or, rather, they are completely exempt from it, as we showed in the case of women, the governed and wild animals. Third after them is this, Christ's coming and promising us greater goods now than the ones of which those in the beginning robbed us by sinning. I mean, tell me, why do you grieve? Because Adam by sinning has driven you from paradise? Live a good life, He says, and practice virtue: not paradise but heaven itself I open to you, and I allow you to suffer no dire consequence of the disobedience of the first-formed. Do you grieve because he lost you government of the wild animals? See, I am subjecting even the demons to you if you pay attention. Scripture says, remember, "Tread on snakes and scorpions and on all the power of the foe" – not "Govern" but "Tread on," hinting at a developed form of government. Hence Paul also said not, "God will put Satan under your feet," but "God will crush Satan under your feet." It is no longer a case of what was said previously, "He shall watch for your head, and you shall watch for your heel;"[15] rather, total the victory, unstained the trophy, complete the enemy's annihilation, his crushing and ruin. Eve subjected you to her husband, whereas I make you equal in status not only to her husband but also the angels, if you want it. He stripped you of the present life, whereas I grant you also the future life, ageless and unending, replete with countless good things. Let no one think themselves undone by our first parents. If we are prepared to reach on all he is ready to provide, we shall find what is given much more than we lost.

From what has been said the rest is also clear. Adam ushered in a harsh way of living; Christ promises us life whence pain and grief and groaning have departed, and He pledges to gift us with the kingdom of heaven. "Come now, you blessed of my Father," He says, remember, "inherit the kingdom prepared for you from the foundation of the world. For I was hungry and you gave me something to eat, I was thirsty and you gave me a drink, I was a stranger and you brought me in, I was naked and you clothed me, in prison and you came to see me." [16] Shall we, too, hear that beatitude? I would not be so sure: our neglect of the poor is extreme. It is the time of fasting, such close attention and much instruction in salutary doctrines, constant praying, daily assemblies – and the outcome of such devotion? Nothing. From here we go off, seeing the clusters of the poor drawn up on all sides; with a glance at them as though they were pillars and not human bodies we pass them by pitilessly; with a glance at them as though they were lifeless statues and not breathing human beings (603) we hurry off home.

Hunger obliges me to, you claim. Would that hunger persuaded you to stay. Full stomachs, the proverb says, know nothing of empty ones, whereas empty ones recognize another from experience of their own need – or, rather, not even then is it possible to grasp it fully. I mean, while you betake yourself to a carefully-laid table, not prepared to wait even a little, the poor person stands still right up till evening, anxious and desperate to get enough food for the day; and when he sees the day over without all the money collected that is needed for his daily sustenance, he is reduced to regrets and recriminations, and is led to take measures beyond his capabilities. Hence at evening time they beset us more earnestly, appealing, adjuring, weeping and wailing, wringing their hands, forced into countless other shameless gestures. They are afraid, you see, that when everyone has gone home, they are destined to wander the city like a wilderness. And just as people wrecked at sea in the daytime and clinging to a plank exert themselves to reach port before evening in case they are still at sea when night falls and they suffer a worse fate than shipwreck, so too the poor, fearing hunger like shipwreck, try hard before evening to collect enough money for their food, in case, when everyone has gone off home, they remain outside the port – their port being the hands that offer them help. [17]

We for our part, however, are moved by their plight neither in the marketplace nor on our way home. Instead, with our table laid, which is often groaning under countless good things – if we should call good what we eat as an indictment of our inhumanity – with our table laid, and though hearing them below walking through the narrow passages, crying aloud in the streets, grieving in utter gloom, in complete isolation, we are still unmoved. Instead, with stomach full and off to bed, hearing them raising strident laments below even at that time again like a wild dog, we still give no ear to a human voice, but ignore them. We are unaffected by the time, that at that hour of the night with everyone else asleep that person alone is lamenting his lot, or by the trivial nature of the request, that he wants from us nothing more than some bread or a little money, or by the extremity of his plight, that he is always in the grip of hunger, or by the simplicity of the beggar, that though under the effect of such great need he does not presume to approach the door or come near, merely making his request from a great distance. If he receives something, he offers countless prayers; if he receives nothing, he utters no harsh word, neither abuses nor curses those in a position to give but making no offering; instead, like someone being led to unbearable punishment by an executioner, begging and imploring the passersby without receiving any support, (604) taken off to his punishment with great inhumanity, so too this poor person, dragged off to his unbearable vigil at night by hunger like some executioner, stretches out his hands, in a loud cry appealing to those seated upstairs in their homes, but receives no pity and is heartlessly sent on his way with great severity.

None of this moves us, however; instead, we presume to raise our hands to heaven despite such inhumanity, speak to

God about mercy, and beg pardon for our sins, and are not afraid of a thunderbolt striking us after such a prayer, despite such severity and inhumanity. How do we go to bed and rest, tell me, and not fear that the poor man would appear to us in person, dirty and filthy, clad in rags, weeping and wailing, censuring our severity? In fact, I have often heard many people say that, after a day when they neglected to assist the poor, they saw themselves by night enveloped in ropes, dragged off by the hand of the poor to suffer torture and countless other things. That is only sleeping and dreaming, however, a short-lived punishment; in our case, on the other hand, are we not afraid, tell me, of seeing this poor person weeping and wailing and lamenting in the bosom of Abraham, as that wealthy man once saw Lazarus? But at this point I leave to your conscience those harsh and unmitigated punishments, how he begged for water, how he was given not even a drop, how his tongue was tormented, how he made his appeal and gained no pardon, and how he suffered undying punishments. [18]

Let it not be our fate, however, to learn this by experience; instead, on hearing it in word let us avoid the threat of it in fact by proving ourselves worthy of the greeting from our forefather Abraham and be admitted to the same place with him, thanks to the grace and lovingkindness of our Lord Jesus Christ, to whom with the Father and the Holy Spirit be honor, glory and power, now and forever, for ages of ages. Amen.

Sermon Six

In the same text, that before eating from the tree of knowledge Adam knew good and evil,

and on the need to ponder at home what is said in church.

On the one hand, I like fasting because it is the mother of self-control and source of all sound values. On the other, I like it also for your sake and for your good selves for bringing together this sacred assembly of you people, and for making possible the prospect I relish of seeing you again and allowing me to be sure of enjoying this lovely festival and celebration.[1] In fact, one would not be wrong in calling an assembly of your good selves a festival, a celebration and countless good things. After all, if someone goes into the marketplace and on meeting a friend often loses all depression, whereas in our case we meet not in the marketplace but in church, and do not encounter simply a single friend but (605) are in the company of so many wonderful brethren and fathers, how shall we not be relieved of all depression, how not reap complete satisfaction?

In fact, it is not only on the score of number that this congregation is better than the crowds in the marketplace, but also for the actual nature of the communication: crowds meeting in the marketplace and sitting together with one another in a circle often talk about nonsensical maters, get involved in idle chatter and give voice to sentiments unbefitting them. It is our custom most of the time, you see, to show greater interest in prying into other people's affairs and busying ourselves with them.[2] That it is a dangerous and risky business to give vent and give ear to such sentiments and be taken in by them, and that many storms are often generated in homes through such gatherings, I pass over for the time being; but no one would deny that all that talk is nonsensical, silly and worldly, and that no spiritual topic would ever be readily raised in such an assembly.

Here, on the contrary, it is not like that: quite the opposite. In fact, all useless talk is expelled, only spiritual instruction is allowed in. We are discussing our soul, you see, the good things befitting the soul, the crowns stored up in heaven, illustrious lives, God's lovingkindness, His care for everything, and all other things particularly befitting us, why we were made, what fate awaits us after our departure from here, and what our situation will be then. It is not ourselves alone who participate in this assembly, but prophets and apostles as well – and the greatest thing of all, in our midst there stands Jesus, the Lord of all, in person. It was He, remember, who said, "Where two or three are gathered together in my name, there am I in the midst of them." [3] But if where two or three are gathered together, He is in their midst, much more where so many men, so many women, so many fathers, and apostles and prophets are present.

Hence, enjoying grace from that source, we speak with greater enthusiasm and keep the promise made to you. We promised, remember, to speak first about the tree, whether knowledge of good and evil came to Adam from it, or he had this discernment even before eating. [4] We would therefore now confidently say that he had this discernment even before eating: if he had not known what was good and what was evil, he would have been more irrational than the irrational animals, the master would have been more foolish than the slave. After all, how would it not be absurd for goats and sheep to know which plants are good for them, which harmful, and instead of staying at the surface level to have discernment and a clear knowledge of what is injurious to them and what useful, whereas the human being is deprived of such certainty? If he did not have it, in fact, he would be worth nothing, and would even be of lower status than all others. (606) I mean, it would have been more desirable for him to live in darkness, with eyes put out and deprived of light, than not to know what is good and what is evil. After all, if you took this from our life, you would destroy our life completely and fill everything with utter confusion, this being the thing in which we differ from brute beasts and by which we are better than animals, by knowing evil and virtue, recognizing what is wicked and not being in ignorance of what is good.

If we now know this, however, and not just we ourselves but also Scythians and savages,[5] much more did that human being know it at that time before sin. The one endowed with such honors, like being made "in the image" and "in the likeness" of God and the other blessings, would not have remained deprived of their summit: only those creatures are ignorant of good and evil who by nature are deprived of intelligence, whereas Adam was filled with complete wisdom and was capable of distinguishing each of them. For proof that he was filled with spiritual wisdom, listen to this: *God brought the animals to him to see what he would call them; and what Adam called them became their name.* So consider how much wisdom it was with which he was filled in being able to give names to so many genera, so many different species – cattle, reptiles, birds – all properly applied. God, in fact, so far accepted the naming as never to change those names, or even remove their names when he sinned. *Whatever Adam called them*, the text says, *was their name.* [6] Was he, at any rate, ignorant of what is good and what is evil? What basis is there for that?

Again, he brought the woman to him, and on seeing her he immediately recognized what he had in common with her by nature. What did he say? *This is now bone of my bones and flesh of my flesh.* Since God a little before had been presenting all the animals to him, you see, Adam wanted to show that this being was not one of those beings, and said, *This is now bone of my bones and flesh of my flesh*. Now, some commentators claim that he is suggesting not simply that fact but also the manner of Creation, and that by saying *This is now* he suggests that such a genesis would not apply to a woman as well – the meaning given by another translator as well in rendering it more precisely "This once," as if to say, Only now is a woman made from a man alone, whereas later it will not be in this manner but from both.[7] *Bone from my bones and flesh from my flesh*: God took one piece from the whole mass and formed the woman in such a way that she would have everything in common with the man, the text saying, *She will be called woman because she was taken from the man*. Do you see how he also gives the name with intention of having the name convey the commonality in nature, and the manner of Creation being the basis of constant love and bond of (607) harmony?

What does He say next? *For this reason*

a person will leave his father and his mother, and cling to his wife. He did not say *will be united* but *will cling to* so as to bring out the precise attachment. *And the two will become one flesh.* [8] Did the one who knew this, tell me, not know what is good and what is evil? How would you account for that? After all, if instead of knowing what is good and what is evil before eating from the tree, he learnt it after eating, sin would have been his teacher in wisdom, and the serpent would have proved not deceiver but adviser in what was advantageous, turning him from a beast into a human being. [9] Perish the thought; it was not like that, not like that. I mean, if he had not known what was good and what was evil, how was he the recipient of the commandment? No one, after all, gives a law to someone not aware that transgression of it is wrong, whereas God both gave it and punished him as a transgressor, neither of which He would have done unless from the beginning He made him aware of virtue and vice. Do you see how it is made clear to us from all angles that instead of his knowing good and evil after eating from the tree, he understood before this as well?

Let us take all this to heart, then, dearly beloved, and on returning home let us serve a double meal, one of food and the other of sacred reading; while the husband reads what has been said, let the wife learn and the children listen, and let not even servants be deprived of the chance to listen. Turn your house into a church; you are, in fact, even responsible for the salvation both of the children and of the servants. Just as we are accountable for you, so too each of you is accountable for your servant, your wife, your child. [10] In the wake of such stories sweet dreams will befall you, rid of every nightmare; all that the soul is in the habit of pondering on during the day becomes the stuff of our dreams in sleep. If we keep hold of what is said each day, we shall not need effort: the sermon afterwards will be clearer and the teaching on our part more enthusiastic. In order, then, that there be some further benefit for us and for you – for us from teaching, for you from listening – let a spiritual meal be set before you after the material meal; it will bring you security and adornment, God will direct the things of this life to your benefit, and everything will be very simple and easy for you. Scripture says, remember, "Seek first the kingdom of heaven, and all this will come to you as well." [11] Seek it, then, dearly beloved, so that we may attain to the good things both here and there, thanks to the grace and lovingkindness of our Lord Jesus Christ, through whom and with whom be glory to the Father and the Holy Spirit, now and forever, for ages of ages. Amen.

SERMON SEVEN

*In the same text, why is the tree called "tree
of the knowledge of good and evil"?*

*And what is the meaning of the verse,
"Today you will be with me in paradise"?*

Yesterday I urged your good selves to
remember what was said and in the
evening serve a double (608) meal, add-
ing to the food a feast from the words.
Well, then, did you do it – serve a double
meal? I know you did, partaking not only
of the former but also the latter. In fact, in
your concern for the lesser one, you would
not have been likely to neglect the better
one, the latter being better than the former:
while the hands of cooks assembled the
former, tongues of inspired authors prepared the latter. One boasts the produce
of the earth, the other a crop from the

Spirit; food from the former table has a rapid course to corruption, but from the latter to incorruption; the former contributes to our present life, the latter guides us to the future one. Your serving the one with the other, then, I am aware of, not from asking your attendant, not your servant, but the messenger clearer than they. Which one was that? The applause for my words, the commendation for my teaching: when I said yesterday, Let each of you turn your home into a church, you burst into loud applause, indicating satisfaction with what was said. [1] Now, the person who with satisfaction listens to what is said is also ready for demonstration in action. Hence today as well I have girded myself more enthusiastically for teaching.

Arouse yourselves now, too. It is, in fact, not only the speaker who should be aroused: the listeners should also be alert – the listeners more than the speaker. I mean, while we have a single concern, to deposit the Lord's goods, in your case the task is greater, to accept them and preserve

them very securely. After listening, therefore, put locks and bars on the doors; sta-
tion fearsome thoughts like guards everywhere in your soul. The thief is shameless, in fact, always on the watch, and constantly on the attack; even if he often fails,
he often tries his hand. So let the guards
be fearsome: if they see the devil entering
with the intention of snatching some of
what is deposited, let them drive him off
with a loud cry; if worldly worries make
an assault, let them obstruct them; if natural forgetfulness proves a problem, let
them stimulate the memory with practice.
The risk of losing the master's possessions, you see, is not slight: people who
receive these possessions and squander
what is entrusted to them are often punished with death; so what punishment
would be imposed on those who receive
the sayings – a much more valuable trust
than that – and then lose them? In the case
of the former possessions only those who
receive them are liable, no one else, the
obligation being for them to deposit all

they received, and nothing else being required of them; but in the case of God's words we are responsible not only for guarding them but also for much exertion, but ordered not only to pay back what we have received but even to offer this twofold to the Lord. Admittedly, even if there were an obligation only to guard them, that obligation would involve effort and care; (609) but when the Lord bids us make them multiply, consider how much toil and worry is required of us, to whom they have been committed.[2]

This is surely the reason why the person entrusted with five talents brought back not what he had been entrusted with but as much more besides: the five came from the master's lovingkindness, whereas the servant was obliged also to give evidence of his own zeal. Likewise the one entrusted with the two talents produced another two, and hence he was accorded the same honor by his master. But the person who in turn was entrusted with one talent brought back the same amount as he had been entrusted with, not reducing it, not lessening the deposit, not repaying only half; but because he could give no proof of transactions or bring back double what he had been entrusted with, he paid the ultimate penalty. And rightly so: if I had meant, the master says, only for it to be protected and no interest earned on it, I would not have put it into the servants' hands.

For your part, I ask you, observe the master's lovingkindness: the person entrusted with the five talents brought back another five, and with the two as much again, and each of them received the same rewards: just as he said to the former, "Well done, good and faithful servant, you have been faithful in the case of a small amount, I shall put you in charge of a large amount," and he says likewise to the person bringing back the two, "Well done, good and faithful servant, you have been faithful in the case of a small amount, I shall put you in charge of a large amount." The amount was not the same, but the interest was the same, and he accorded the latter the same honor. Why? Because God had regard not to the amount of what was brought back but to the ability of those who produced it. Each of them, in fact, gave evidence of doing his best: it was not indifference on the part of one and zeal on the part of the other that resulted in greater or less returns, but the difference in the deposit. One received five and brought back another five; the other received two and brought back two, which in no respect was less as regards zeal, both men doubling what had been entrusted to them, whereas the man who received on only brought it back – hence, too, his punishment.[3]

Did you hear, then, the awful punishment laid up for those not busying themselves with the master's possessions? Let us therefore both protect them and busy ourselves with them, and give evidence of much trading with them. Let no one claim, I am an ordinary person, I am a learner, I have no role in teaching, unlettered as I am and worth nothing. I mean, even if you are an ordinary person, even if unlettered, even if you have been entrusted with one talent, make the most of what has been committed to you, and you will receive the same reward as the one who teaches you. But while I really believe that you guard what has been said and with great precision hold fast to it, lest we spend the whole sermon on this topic – come now, let us supply the sequel of what was said by us yesterday, thus making you a repayment for your guarding it; the person who was entrusted with something previously and preserved it would deserve to receive other things as well. So what was the story previously communicated to you yesterday? It was the account of the tree, and we proved that the human being knew good and evil before eating of the tree, and he was filled with great wisdom, which enabled him to give the animals names, which enabled him to recognize his wife, which enabled him to say, *This is now bone of* (610) *my bones,* which enabled him to discourse on marriage, on having children, on intercourse and father and mother, which enabled him to be given a commandment. [4] No one, remember, gives to a person ignorant of good and evil a commandment and law about what is to be done and not be done.

Today there is need to explain why, if the human being did not receive the knowledge of good and evil from the tree, it is called the *tree of the knowledge of good and evil*. It is, in fact, not unimportant to learn what was the reason for the tree's having this name. The devil said, remember, *On the day you eat of the tree your eyes will be opened, and you will be like gods, knowing good and evil.* [5] So how do you claim, you ask, that it did not impart a knowledge of good and evil? I mean, tell me, who did impart it? The devil, you reply. Are you thus offering me testimony from the foe and the conspirator? Admittedly he said, *And you will be gods*: surely, therefore, they did not also become gods? Just as they did not become gods, then, so neither was it at that time that they gained a knowledge of good and evil; he is in fact a liar, speaking nothing that is true, Scripture saying, "He does not stand in the truth." [6] Far from adducing testimony from the foe, let us see from the events themselves why it is referred to as *the tree of the knowledge of good and evil*. First, if you do not mind, let us consider what is good and evil. So what is good? Obedience. And what is evil? Disobedience. For the time being, in case we are deceived about the nature of good and evil, let us examine this question from the Scriptures, listening to what the prophet says on the question of good and evil: "What is good? And what does the Lord God require of you other than acting justly and loving mercy?" Do you see that obedience is good, obedience coming from love? And again, "This people of mine did two wicked things: they abandoned me, source of living water, and dug for themselves broken cisterns unable to hold water." Do you see that disobedience and abandonment are evil?[7]

Let us hold on to that fact, then, that obedience is good and disobedience evil, and we shall thus understand the former case as well. The tree is referred to as the *knowledge of good and evil*, in fact, for the reason that the commandment exercising them in obedience and disobedience was given in regard to the tree: while Adam knew before this that obedience was good and disobedience evil, he learnt it more clearly later from actual experience. Cain likewise, in fact, knew that killing one's brother is wrong even before he slew his brother; for proof that he knew the action was evil, listen to what he says: "Come now, let us go out into the countryside." Why, pray, does he snatch his brother from his parents' arms and entice him out into the countryside? Why put him in an isolated area? Why deprive him of assistance? Why remove him far from the sight of his father? Why conceal the deed if he was not aghast at his sin? Why after committing the murder did he quibble and lie when asked again? (611) When God asked, remember, "Where is Abel your brother?" you replied, "Surely I am not my brother's keeper?"[8] It is clear from this that he was clearly aware when he embarked on this deed. Just as this man was aware even before experience that murder was wrong, therefore, but learned it more clearly after as well when he received the punishment and heard the words, "You will be groaning and trembling on the earth,"[9] so too his father had knowledge of good and evil even before eating, even if not as clearly as after eating from the tree.

What is my drift? We all know what is wrong even before doing it, but we learn it more clearly after doing it – and much more clearly when we are punished. Thus Cain also knew that murdering one's brother is wrong even beforehand, but later learned it more clearly through being punished. While we also know even before experience that health is good and sickness a nuisance, much more do we come to know the difference in the two when we fall sick. In just the same way Adam knew that obedience is good and disobedience wrong, but he later learned it more clearly when he was expelled from the garden for tasting fruit from the tree, and forfeited that blessed state. Since he fell foul of punishment for tasting fruit from the tree despite God's veto, then, the punishment taught him more clearly how wrong it is to disobey God and how good to obey – hence the tree's being called *knowledge of good and evil*. Why is it that, if the very nature of the tree did not contain the knowledge of good and evil, and instead the human being learned it more clearly from punishment for disobedience in regard to the tree, the tree is called *knowledge of good and evil*? Because this is a custom with Scripture, when an event happens in places or at times, to call the places and times after the events.

For my statement to be clearer, I shall make it obvious with an example. Isaac on one occasion dug a well; the neighboring people tried to destroy the reservoir. This gave rise to enmity, and the well was called Hostility, not that the actual well was hostile but because hostility developed around it. Likewise with the name *tree of the knowledge of good and evil,* not that it contained knowledge but because the proof of the knowledge of good and evil emerged in connection with it. Again, Abraham dug a well, and Abimelech fell to making schemes; they met, resolved the hostility, and after making oaths with one another they called the well Well of the Oath – not that the well made the oath, but because the oath was sworn about the well. Do you see how the places are not responsible for the events, even if taking their names from the events? There is great need, in fact, to adduce examples for the claim to be made clearer. On another occasion Jacob had a vision of angels meeting him and God's camp, and he called the place Camp. [10] Do you see how he called the place after the event occurring in the place? Likewise *the tree of the knowledge of good and evil* is also the name given, not that it had a knowledge of good and evil, but because the proof of the knowledge of good and evil was given in connection with it, as well as exercise in disobedience and obedience. (612) Again Jacob saw God (insofar as it was possible for a human being to see Him), and gave the place the name Sight of God. Why? "Because I have seen God," he said. The place was not actually a sight of God; instead, the name came from the event occurring in the place.[11] Do you see how it is proven from so many examples that it is customary with Scripture to call the actual places after the events occurring in the places? It has the same custom in regard to times as well.

Lest we weary you, however, come now, let us shift the sermon from more depressing matters to the more uplifting; by dwelling on very subtle questions your brains have been wearied. Hence it is good to give them a rest by letting them graze on simpler and more uplifting ideas. Let us return, therefore, to the saving tree of the cross. This tree it is, you see, this it is that undid all the calamities the other brought on – or, rather, it was not it but the human being that brought on all the calamities, which Christ later undid in great abundance by bringing on good things greater than them. Hence Paul says, "Where sin abounded, grace did more abound," that is, the gift was greater than the sin; hence he also says, "The free gift is not like the fall," the human being did not sin to the extent that God gave grace, the loss was not as great as the gain, the shipwreck was not as great as the commerce – instead, the good things outweighed the bad. And rightly so: a slave brought on the bad things, and they were less, whereas the Lord granted the good things – consequently they too were greater; hence his saying, "The free gift is not like the fall." He then goes on to mention the difference as well: "While the judgment following one fall brought on condemnation, the free gift following many falls brings justification." [12]

The statement is obscure; there is therefore need to supply clarification. "The judgment:" the penalty, the punishment, death. "Following one fall:" sin, since while a single sin brought on such dreadful evil, grace undid not only that sin but also other sins. Hence it says, "The free gift following many falls brings justification." For this reason John the Baptist also cried aloud, "Behold the lamb of God," not the one who takes way the sin of Adam, but "who takes away the sin of the world." [13] Do you see how it was a case, not of the gift being like the fall, but of this tree bringing on greater good things than the evils which were brought on at the beginning?

Now, I said this lest you think you have been badly affected by the first human beings. The devil expelled Adam, Christ welcomed the brigand: consider the difference. The former expelled the human being, though he had no sin except one blemish of disobedience; Christ welcomed a brigand into paradise though he was carrying countless burdens of sins. Surely this fact, that he welcomed a brigand into paradise, is not the only marvel, and nothing further? There is also something greater to mention: it is not that He welcomed a brigand, but did so before all the world, including the apostles, to prevent anyone (613) despairing of a welcome or giving up hope of their salvation, once they see the one saddled with countless vices inhabiting the royal courts. Let us see, however, whether the brigand gave evidence of effort and upright deeds and a good yield. Far from his being able to claim even this, he made his way into paradise before the apostles with a mere word, on the basis of faith alone, the intention being for you to learn that it was not so much a case of his sound values prevailing as the Lord's lovingkindness being completely responsible.

What, in fact, did the brigand say? What did he do? Did he fast? Did he weep? Did he tear his garments? Did he display repentance in good time? Not at all: on the cross itself after his utterance he won salvation. Note the rapidity: from cross to heaven, from condemnation to salvation. What were those wonderful words, then? What great power did they have that they brought him such marvelous good things? "Remember me in your kingdom." [14] What sort of word is that? He asked to receive good things, he showed no concern for them in action; but the one who knew his heart paid attention not to the words but to the attitude of mind. People who had the benefit of Old Testament teachings, who saw the signs, who witnessed the wonders, said of Christ, "He has a demon," "He deceives the crowd," [15] whereas the brigand, who heard nothing of Old Testament authors, who saw no miracles, who saw a man nailed to the cross, paid no heed to disgrace, took no notice of dishonor, having regard for his divinity and saying, "Remember me in your kingdom." A remarkable and unique happening: you saw a cross and called to mind a kingdom? What did you see that was worthy of a kingdom? A man crucified, flogged, mocked, accused, spat upon, scourged – is this, tell me, worthy of a kingdom? Do you notice that he saw with the eyes of faith, and did not examine appearances? Hence God did not examine mere words, either; instead, just as the fellow had regard for divinity, so God had regard for the brigand's heart, saying, "This day you will be with me in paradise." [16]

At this point pay attention: an issue arises that is not a chance one, namely, the Manichees, stupid and rabid dogs, presenting an appearance of mildness but having on the inside the savage fury of dogs, wolves in sheep's clothing. Lest you look to appearances, however, examine instead the wild beast hidden within. These people, then, seize upon this passage to claim that Christ said, "Amen, amen, I say to you, this day you will be with me in paradise," so reward of good things has already been made, and resurrection is unnecessary; if the brigand was awarded good things that very day whereas his body has not yet risen even today, there will be no resurrection of the body in future. Surely you have not given thought to what was said, or require that it be said a second time? "Amen, amen, I say to you, this day you will be with me in paradise." You claim that the brigand, then, did not enter paradise with his body: how could he, when his body was not buried, and had not turned to dust, and there is no mention anywhere that Christ raised him up? [17] If He welcomed the brigand, and he enjoyed the good things without his body, clearly there is no resurrection of the body; if there were resurrection of the body, He would not have said, "You will be with me in paradise this day," but on the last day when there is a resurrection of bodies. If He had already welcomed the (614) brigand, and his body stayed outside and decayed, clearly there is no resurrection of bodies.

So much for them; now listen to what

is said by us – or, rather, not by us but by the divine Scripture; it is not our teaching we cite but that of the Holy Spirit. [18] What are you claiming – that the flesh has no share in the crown? But after sharing in the labors, is it to be deprived of the rewards? It exuded more sweat when there was need for engagement in the contest; so is the soul alone to be crowned when the time comes for crowns? Do you not hear Paul's words, "We must take our place before the judgment seat of Christ so that each person may receive recompense for actions done by their bodies, good or evil"? Do you not hear his further words, "This mortal body must put on immortality, and this perishable body put on imperishability"? [19] What is mortal, the soul or the body? Clearly the body: the soul is naturally immortal, the body naturally mortal.

They dismiss much of this, however; yet we establish the connection of what remains with what has been dismissed. The brigand entered paradise, they admit.

The meaning of this? Surely this is not the good things God promised us? Do you not hear what Paul says about those good things, "What eye has not seen, nor ear heard, nor has it entered the human heart"? Eye did see Adam's paradise, however, ear heard, and human heart did get word of it (we spent many days talking about it, remember); so how did the brigand lay hold of it? God did not promise to welcome us into paradise, remember, but into heaven itself; His preaching was not of a kingdom of paradise but of a kingdom of heaven. "He began to preach and say," the text says, remember, "Repent: the kingdom of heaven is at hand," not the kingdom of paradise. [20] In other words, though you lost paradise, God gave you heaven so as to give evidence of His lovingkindness and sting the devil, thus bringing out that even if he concocts countless schemes against the human race, it will do him no good, since God is bringing us to ever greater glory. Though you lost paradise, then, God opened

heaven to you; though you were condemned to temporary labor, you were also
given the honor of eternal life. He bade
the earth bring forth thorns and thistles,
and the soul produced for you the crop of
the Spirit.

Do you see how the gain is greater than
the loss, how the riches are more abun-
dant? [21] To use a parallel example: God
formed the human being from earth and
water, and set him in paradise. The one
who was formed did not turn out well,
going astray. From then on He forms them
no longer from earth and water, but from
water and Spirit; He promises them no
longer paradise but the kingdom of
heaven. To learn how this is, listen care-
fully. Nicodemus, remember, leader of the
Jews, having fallen into error, was inquir-
ing about birth at this point and saying
that it was impossible for an old person
to be born again. Notice how Christ very
clearly reveals to him the style of birth,
"Unless someone is born of water and
Spirit, they will not be (615) able to enter

the kingdom of heaven."[22] So if He promised the kingdom of heaven, and welcomed the brigand into paradise, He had not yet repaid him with the good things.

In response to this they make another claim: the paradise He means here is not paradise; instead, He used the term paradise for the kingdom of heaven. Since He was speaking to a brigand, you see, a person who had heard nothing of elevated doctrines, was not aware of inspired writing, and instead had spent his whole life in isolation, committing murders, casting not even a glance at a church or participating in sacred reading, unaware of what the kingdom of heaven is, He put it this way, "This day you will be with me in paradise," suggesting by the better-known and more familiar term "paradise" the kingdom of heaven – this it was of which Christ was talking to him. I follow. Therefore, they say, he entered the kingdom of heaven. What is the proof for that? From His saying, "This day you shall be with me in paradise."

Now, if this solution is rather forced, we shall adduce a clearer one. What is it, then? Christ said, "The one who does not believe in the Son has already been condemned." How so, "already condemned"? Admittedly there was no resurrection at that stage, likewise no penalty or punishment – so how "already condemned"? On the basis of sin. Again, "The one who believes in the Son has transferred from death to life." He did not say, He will transfer, but "He has transferred," once again on the basis of right behavior, as the other in turn was on the basis of sin. Just as the one man is condemned without being judged, therefore, and the other has transferred to life without transferring, and He is speaking to one on the basis of right behavior and to the other on the basis of sin, as though things have occurred that have not yet occurred, so He spoke also to the brigand. Physicians, you see, when they notice someone in a desperate condition, say that he is already dead and buried, even though they can see he is still breathing. Just as such a person, however, with no hope of survival, is dead in the eyes of the physicians, so too the brigand, with no further expectation of relapsing into ruin, entered heaven. Adam likewise heard the words, *On the day you eat of the tree you shall surely die.* So what happened: did he die that day? Not at all: he lived more than nine hundred years after that day. [23] So what did God mean, *You shall surely die*? As a sentence, not in actual experience. In similar fashion the brigand, too, entered heaven. Listen, at any rate, to what Paul says to suggest that no one at that stage had laid hold of the reward of good things: after speaking of the biblical authors and righteous people, he went on, "All of these died in faith without having received the promises, but from a distance they saw and greeted them, since God had provided something better for us so that they would not be made perfect apart from us." [24]

Hold fast to this and remember it; much has been said, and my longing is that you would enjoy a better teaching. [25] Holding fast to it with precision, then, let us prepare ourselves for what is yet to be said by one and all sending up glory to God, to whom be the glory and the power, now and forever, for ages of ages. Amen.

Sermon Eight

In the same text, on the stormy weather, on the assembly of bishops, on the giving of the commandment to Adam, and the fact that being given the law was a mark of great solicitude.

While the build-up of clouds has rendered the day rather gloomy for us, the presence of the teacher has made it brighter. The sun, after all, when sending its beams from its zenith in the midst of the clouds, does not shed light on our bodies to the extent that the countenance of paternal affection gives light to our souls by shedding its beams from the throne. As he is well aware, then, he has not visited us by himself: he has come bringing with him a group of luminaries so that the light may be stronger. Hence our assembly also rejoices, the flocks exult, and we ourselves commence the sermon with greater enthusiasm. After all, where there is a concourse of shepherds, there security for the flocks is also guaranteed; likewise sailors rejoice when they have many pilots with them: when there is peace and calm, they lighten the work of rowing for them by use of the rudders, and when the sea is stirred up, they offset the impact of the waves through their skill and employment of many hands. [1]

Hence we too are confident in developing our sermon in the task of instruction, leaving everything to their prayers. For the message to be clearer and easier for you to grasp, however, we shall also briefly remind you of what was said to you yesterday. I said that the human being knew good and evil before eating from the tree, and that he did not gain this knowledge after tasting. I explained why it was called *tree of the knowledge of good and evil*, and how it is customary with Scripture, when something happens in connection with some place or time, to call the place or time after the event. Today we have to read the actual commandment by which he forbade the eating from the tree. What is it, then? *The Lord God commanded Adam in the words, From every tree in the garden you may eat food.*[2] The law is from God: pay attention. After all, if when people read out an edict from the emperor, they bring the whole audience to their feet, much more ought we, when on the point of reading out laws not of men but of God, be alert in mind and pay heed to the contents.[3]

I am aware that some people find fault with the lawgiver, claiming that the law was responsible for the Fall.[4] It is therefore necessary firstly to take a stand on this and show from the facts themselves that it was not out of hatred for the human being or from a wish to weigh down our nature that He gave the law, but from love and concern. For proof in fact that He gave it to us as an aid listen to what Isaiah says, "For he gave the law as a help;" now, someone who has hatred does not help. Again, the inspired author cries aloud, "Your law is a lamp for my feet and a light for my steps;" now, someone who has hatred does not dissipate the darkness with a lantern, or guide the lost with a light. Again, Solomon, "The commandment of the law is lamp, a light, life, censure and correction." See, it is not only a help, not only a lantern, but also light and life; these things are not from someone who has hatred or from someone who intends to bring ruin, but from someone wanting to stretch out a hand and lift you up. Hence Paul also, in rebutting the Jew and showing the great benefit the law introduced, and the fact that it is not a weight on our nature but a relief, said, "See, you call yourself a Jew and rely on the law." [5]

Do you see that God gave the law not to weigh down our nature but to relieve it? Do you want to see that His intention was also to honor it? These texts in particular, then, also suffice to bring out the honor and the care; yet we shall make the same thing clear from other texts as well. "Praise the Lord, Jerusalem, praise your God, Zion; because He strengthened the bars of your gates, He blessed your children within you – He who put peace as your outer limits and fills you with finest wheat." Then, after mentioning as well the beneficence shown by God in the rest of creation, He went on to a special and greater one in these terms, "He who sends out His word to Jacob, His ordinances and judgments to Israel. He did not act in that way with every nation, nor show them His judgments." [6] Note how many good things He listed: security of the city ("He strengthened the bars of your gates"), freedom from wars ("He who put peace as your outer limits"), abundance (618) of necessities ("He filled you with finest wheat"). Yet He showed the gift of the law to be more precious than all these: a far greater gift than security, peace, freedom from wars, healthy children, large families, and an abundance of necessities is to be given the law, to learn God's ordinances. After imposing it later than all the others as the summit connecting the good things, He went on, "He did not act in that way with every nation." Which way is that? In fact, a great number of them did in many cases enjoy abundance and the other goods listed. I am not referring to the above-mentioned things, however, but to the law, in which respect "he did not act in that way with every nation." Hence his proceeding, "nor show them his judgments."

Do you see how the law is greater than all the goods that are listed? This is a point made also by Jeremiah: in lamenting those in captivity he said, "Why is that you are in the land of the foe? You have forfeited the fountain of wisdom," meaning the law. Just as the fountain releases many streams in all directions, so too the law produces many commandments coursing in all directions to irrigate our soul. Then, to bring out the special honor due to the law, he went on, "This wisdom was not heard of in Canaan, nor seen in Teman, nor did descendants of Hagar, the merchants or the seekers know its ways or remember its paths." And to bring out that it is something spiritual and divine, he says, "Who has gone up to heaven and forced it to come down?"[7] He then went on, "This is our God, no other can be compared to him; he found the whole way to knowledge, and gave her to Jacob his servant and to Israel, beloved by him." Hence David also said, "He did not act like this with every nation, nor show them His judgments." It was this, at any rate, that Paul also was hinting at in writing, "What advantage has the Jew, then? Or what is the value of circumcision?"[8] Much in every way: firstly, they were entrusted with God's sayings. Do you see how he also gave an interpretation of the verse, "He did not act like this with every nation, nor show them his judgments"? In other words, if this is the Jew's advantage, that they alone of all people were honored with the gift of the law in writing,[9] it was surely not to weigh upon our nature but to honor it that God gave the law. And He honored them, not only in this way, by giving them the law, but also by giving it in person: this is the highest form of honor, not simply providing it.

That it is a great gift, in fact, listen to Paul pointing out as much: on seeing the Jews puffed up by the thought of the prophets coming to them, he aims at repressing their conceit in writing in some such terms to the Hebrews to show that we enjoyed a greater honor in being granted instruction not through a slave but through the Master: "In various ways and in various forms in former times God spoke to our forefathers, but in the final days He has spoken to us through a Son." And again elsewhere, "Not only that: we boast in God through our Lord Jesus Christ, through whom we have now also received reconciliation." Do you observe him boasting not (619) only of reconciliation, but also of receiving reconciliation through Christ? And again in celebrating the resurrection he says, "The Lord himself will descend from heaven." [10] Notice how there everything happens through the Lord, and here not through some servant, not through angel or archangel: He personally by Himself commanded Adam, honoring the human being with a double honor, both by giving the law and by giving it personally. How is it, then, that he fell? By his own indifference – something made clear by all who received a law and did not fall, performing instead even more than they were commanded. [11]

Since, however, I see the time pressing upon us, I shall carry the treatment over to another sermon. For your part, for the time being hold on to what was said, remember it, and teach it to those who have not heard it. Let everyone meditate on it in church, in the marketplace and at home; nothing is sweeter than attention to the divine sayings. Listen, at any rate, to what the inspired author says of this, "Your sayings are like honey in my throat, better than honey and the honeycomb in my mouth." [12] So place this honeycomb on

your table at evening so as to fill it completely with spiritual sweetness. Have you
not noticed how affluent people bring in
harpists and flute players after the meal?
They turn their house into an auditorium;
for your part turn your house into heaven,
doing so not by altering the walls or
changing the foundations, but by inviting
the Lord of heaven to your table. God is
not ashamed to be at such meals: in that
setting there is spiritual teaching, there
also sobriety, gravity and simplicity, there
husband and wife and children, harmony
and friendship, people linked by the
bonds of virtue, there in the midst is
Christ. It is not a roof of gold He looks for,
in fact, nor gleaming columns, nor beautiful marble figures – rather, charm of soul,
beauty of mind, a table groaning with
righteousness and containing the fruits of
almsgiving. If He sees such a table, He
quickly joins the party and takes His place,
having said in His own words, "You saw
me hungry and fed me." [13]

When you hear a poor person below

shouting out at the top of his voice, therefore, and then you give the beggar something from the table's dishes, you have invited the Master to your table in the person of the slave, filling it with blessings, and through the first fruits providing the best occasion of making your inner chambers abound with good things. May the God of peace and love, who gives bread for eating and seed to the sower,[14] multiply your yield and give increase to your produce of righteousness in every respect by giving grace from Him, and may He gift us with the kingdom of heaven. May it be the good fortune of us all to attain this, thanks to the grace and lovingkindness of our Lord Jesus Christ, to whom with the Father and the Holy Spirit be glory, honor and power, now and forever, for ages of ages. Amen.

SELECT BIBLIOGRAPHY

Barthélemy, D., *Les Devanciers d'Aquila*, *VTS* X, Leiden, 1963

Baur, P. C., *John Chrysostom and his Time*, 2 vols, Eng. trans., London-Glasgow, 1959,1960

Bouyer, L., *The Spirituality of the New Testament and the Fathers*, Eng. trans., London, 1963

Brottier, L., *Jean Chrysostome. Sermons sur la Genèse*, SC 433, 1998

Dahood, M., "Ebla, Ugarit and the Old Testament," *The Month* 239 (1978) 271-76,341-45

Drewery, B., "Antiochien," *TRE* 3, 103-113

Fernandez Marcos, N., *The Septuagint in Context: Introduction to the Greek Versions of the Bible*, Eng. trans., Boston-Leiden, 2001

de Ghellinck, J., *Patristique et moyen age. Etudes d'histoire littéraire et doctrinale*, 2 *Introductions et compléments à l'étude de la patristique*, Paris, 1947

Hill, R. C., "*Akribeia*: a principle of Chrysostom's exegesis," *Colloquium* 14 (Oct. 1981) 32-36

__________ , "Chrysostom's terminology for

the inspired Word," *EstBíb* 41 1983) 367-73

__________ , *St John Chrysostom's Homilies on Genesis*, FOTC 74,82,87, 1986, 1990, 1992

__________ , "Psalm 45: a *locus classicus* for patristic thinking on biblical inspiration," *StudP* 25 (1991) 95-100

__________ , "The spirituality of Chrysostom's *Commentary on the Psalms*," *JECS* 5 (1997) 569-79

__________ , "Chrysostom's Commentary on the Psalms: homilies or tracts?" in P. Allen et al (edd.), *Prayer and Spirituality in the Early Church* I, Brisbane 1998

__________ , "A pelagian commentator on the Psalms?" *ITQ* 65 (1998) 263-71

__________ , *St John Chrysostom. Commentary on the Psalms*, 2 vols, Brookline MA, 1998

__________ , "Chrysostom's homilies on David and Saul," *SVTQ* 44 (2000) 123-41

__________ , "'Norms, definitions and unalterable doctrines': Chrysostom on Jeremiah," *ITQ* 65 (2000) 335-46

__________ , "St John Chrysostom's homilies on Hannah," *SVTQ* 45 (2001) 319-38

__________ , "Chrysostom on the obscurity of the Old Testament," *OCP* 67 (2001) 371-83

__________ , *St John Chrysostom. Old Testament Homilies*, 3 vols, Brookline MA, 2003

Kelly, J. N. D., *Early Christian Doctrines*, 5th ed., New York, 1978

__________ , *Golden Mouth. The Story of John Chrysostom. Ascetic, Preacher, Bishop*, Ithaca NY, 1995

Leroux, J.-M., "Johannes Chrysostomus," *TRE* 17, 118-27

Marcowicz, W. A., "Chrysostom's sermons on *Genesis*: a problem," *TS* 24 (1963) 652-64

Mayer, W., Allen, P., *John Chrysostom*, The Early Church Fathers, London-New York, 2000

van de Paverd, F., *The Homilies on the Statues. An Introduction*, OCA 239, Rome, 1991

von Rad, G., *Genesis*, Eng. trans., Old Testament Library, rev. ed., London, 1972

Schäublin, C., "Diodor von Tarsus," *TRE* 8, 763-67

__________ , *Untersuchungen zu Methode und Herkunft der Antiochenischen Exegese*, Theophaneia: Beiträge zur Religions- und Kirchengeschichte des Altertums 23, Köln-Bonn, 1974

Speiser, E. A., *Genesis*, Anchor Bible 1, Garden City NY, 1964

Wallace-Hadrill, D. S., *Christian Antioch. A Study of Early Christian Thought in the East*, Cambridge, 1982
Young, F., *Biblical Exegesis and the Formation of Christian Culture*, Cambridge, 1997

Notes

Sermon One

[1] The title, obviously not the author's, occurs in many mss; its accuracy depends on the scribe. Reasons for not rendering the reference in this Lenten material to Quadragesima as "Lent" (an eight-week period in that church) are given in the introduction. Though as noted there also the translation is of the Greek text in the critical edition by Laurence Brottier (SC 433), numbers of columns of the edition in PG 54 (reprinted from Bernard De Montfaucon's eighteenth-century ed.) have been inserted into the text for convenience.

[2] Prov 1:9. As a good preacher, Chrysostom roots his parenesis in (conventional) imagery familiar to his readers. Brottier prefers to take the verb φιλοσοφεῖν, rendered above as having sound values, in the sense here of engaging in Christian meditation. A little further on, the verb (which can have a range of meanings) is used in the sense of exercising one's mind.

[3] Wis 13:5 (one of the deuterocanonical books in Chrysostom's canon). Genesis was a traditional Lenten text, which Chrysostom will treat again in the longer series of Homilies a couple of years later. As usual, the text for the day was first read aloud before the preacher's λόγος.

[4] Antiochene precision, ἀκρίβεια, which has many applications, for one thing prevents confusion of impor-

tant theological distinctions (as also in dogmatic formulation like the Chalcedonian formula). Chrysostom sees Manicheans and Ἕλληνες (in the sense of "pagans") both guilty of this confusion; but did the Manicheans in fact exalt, and not rather deny, the value of created matter?

[5] Rom 1:25.

[6] Isa 1:16-18.

[7] Isa 43:26.

[8] Chrysostom is convinced of the divine inspiration of the biblical authors (Moses for one, as author of the Pentateuch) by a process of personal communication, ὁμιλία. The notion of these authors delivering a scriptural form of this communication as letters Chrysostom will also employ elsewhere. (The point is made in exactly the same form in his second homily on Gen, whereas in Sermon 8 an imperial edict is the figure employed.)

[9] Gen 1:1. This immediate move to address a possible interjection about the angels we find also in Theodoret's *Questions on Genesis* (probably with Chrysostom open before him), who also tells us about the widespread cult of the angels in Antioch communities.

[10] Ps 148:1-2.

[11] Acts 17:24; Col 1:16; Jn 1:3. We cannot fault a preacher for confusing one Pauline letter with another, though when Chrysostom comes to cite the same texts again in Homily 2 he (or his stenographer) corrects the slip.

[12] Ps 33:9. Elsewhere also Chrysostom and the other Antioch Fathers will speak of the relationship of the two Testaments (on the basis of divine inspiration of authors both προφητικοί and ἀποστολικοί); his conception of it here is in terms of more or less developed theology be-

fitting more or less advanced recipients, τέλειοι. Pejorative he may be about the latter, never about the former.
[13] Chrysostom is using Γραφή here in the sense used in the New Testament, that is, the Old Testament, which the Manicheans and Marcionites did not accept. So he is obliged – and happy – to conduct his argument on the basis of human experience.
[14] Chrysostom, whose physiology rests on the theory of the four bodily humors, also bases his argument on alchemy, by which gold is a human product of the metallurgist's skill. But his case stands nonetheless.
[15] Wis 9:14. Chrysostom's aggressive attitude to Manichean, Marcionite and gnostic beliefs on material creation suggests the danger these represented at the time. Montfaucon notes at this point: "Mani, Marcion and Valentinus denied that God is a creator. Mani claimed that matter is eternal, his book beginning (on the authority of Epiphanius), 'God and matter exist, light and darkness.' Marcion accepted two principles, good and evil, saying that the good God created nothing in the world. Valentinians attributed everything to the aeons." By way of antidote Chrysostom offers his congregation Genesis 1:1 as a mantra.
[16] Gen 1:2. Where the Hebrew has the quaint phrase *tohu wabohu* the LXX reads the former element, which means formless, as "invisible," ἀόρατος, which looks like a scribal error for ἀόριστος. Chrysostom is not in a position to critique the text before him, nor does he consult alternative versions; in fact, he seems to be reading both terms, as the Hebrew intends, in the sense of incompleteness (as also in Homily 2). His following rationale does not include a reference to primeval chaos arising from earlier mythologies reflected in the Hebrew, pre-

dictably; the commentator is again thinking of aberrations of his own time.

[17] Matt 5:16. Chrysostom proceeds to propose his bishop Flavian, present in church, as a model of almsgiving (giving the sermon an "appearance of actuality," in Baur's term, not found in the homilies).

[18] 1 Cor 2:9; cf Isa 64:4. For the Antiochenes ῥᾳθυμία, "indifference, neglect, sloth," is the capital sin – the sin of the first parents, Chrysostom claims in the homilies. Its correlative is προθυμία, "enthusiasm, zeal."

[19] Cf Luke 21:1-4. Perhaps because Chrysostom agreed to joust with adversaries on their own terms and not on a scriptural basis, scriptural cross-referencing has been unusually sparse. The sermon concludes with the doxology (in customary form except for mention of the priests, omitted in some mss; cf. opening to next sermon). The preacher has not covered much of the Genesis text; but with this being annual fare, he feels justified in using it to serve his own agenda: exegesis/commentary is not his basic aim. The brevity of the sermon compared, say, with those on the Psalms given in a classroom setting is perhaps accounted for by the presence of (at least) the bishop, who may also have spoken.

Sermon Two

[1] Chrysostom refers to the first homily as being delivered not "yesterday" but "the other day," πρώην.

[2] Chrysostom employs this figure of the speaker's tongue as a sail in his fourth homily on Isaiah 6, a series known as *In Oziam*, where it is not prayer but the inspiration of the Spirit that fills the sail. For the presence of clergy at these sermons, see note 19 on the first homily

above; cf.also the phrase below "brethren and fathers."
³ Gen 1:26. (The PG text at this point reads, "Since it
was the size of the venue that forced us …") It is not
only the apposite character of the similes that
Chrysostom adopts to involve his congregation and
their being sustained to Homeric lengths that appeals
to a reader, but also his careful observation of such a
secular pastime. The preacher is obviously no stranger
to the stadium – unlike the theatre and the races, which
he finds so morally reprehensible (Augustine in the West
concurring).
⁴ Cf. Jn 3:16; Rom 8:32.
⁵ Cf. Eph 2:6.
⁶ Jn 5:46. Chrysostom, like other Fathers, has Pauline
support (cf. 2 Cor 3-4) for claiming that while the OT is
Jewish in origin, Christians can recognize its proper
sense (from guidance within its own pages, some
Antiochenes would claim).
⁷ Isa 6:1-2 (verses on which Chrysostom delivered a series of homilies). Again there is need by the speaker to
address popular sensitivity to the role of angels.
⁸ The notion of God's συγκατάβασις, "considerateness,"
(not, *pace* Brottier and many other commentators, "con-
descension," there being nothing patronizing in the divine willingness to take into account limitations human
or angelic) Chrysostom will invoke more generally of
the considerateness exemplified in the language of the
Scriptures.
⁹ Cf. Isa 9:6 in the Antioch form of the LXX (see Introduction for Chrysostom's text). So finally, faced with
this plural verb, a *crux interpretum* in which a modern
commentator on Genesis like Ephraim Speiser will see
vestiges of a royal plural (a question of "grammar alone,

with no bearing on meaning"), Chrysostom hints at a trinitarian interpretation, as will Theodoret later in his *Quaestiones*.

[10] Chrysostom maintains that the pronoun refers not to first person singular, nor to second person singular or plural (an English translation is unable to register this), but to first person plural.

[11] The "other" commentators whose views Chrysostom also rejects, beyond the Jews, may include Origen with his idea of a pre-cosmic Fall and the gnostic writers attributing a creative role to a demiurge (Theodoret in his *Quaestiones* canvassing a wide range of alternative views). Chrysostom's notion of image and likeness as the human being's governing role has received support from modern archeologists, specifically at Ebla, where (Mitchell Dahood tells us) tablets were unearthed containing lists of deities among which occurs the term *dimutu*, an early form of Heb. *demuth*, "likeness" – in other words, the human being is appointed to act a deputy deity in managing creation. The richness of the notion (as modern cosmologists and conservationists might exploit) Chrysostom does not develop.

[12] 1 Cor 11:7,10; Gen 3:16. There is something of a sleight of hand going on in Chrysostom's reading of Genesis 1:26 to see government assigned to the male alone, the generic term ἄνθρωπος in his text being read in the sense of the gender-specific term ἀνήρ – with encouragement from Paul, he implies, though in that Corinthian context Paul is skewing Jewish tradition (and Genesis 1:27) to underline female inferiority, on which Chrysostom will capitalize again in Sermon Four. (It appears that, as usual, he is addressing himself to men, even if a case can be made for women's also being in attendance.)

[13] Acts 17:29. We were made in the image of God, Chrysostom is saying; we should not make God in our image.

[14] Matt 7:21.

Sermon Three

[1] The preacher is obviously not concerned to move quickly through the book of Genesis; he indulges in some (conventional) imagery to make the point that he going to elaborate on the same verse (1:26ff) to which the previous homily was devoted. He presumes that the congregation is the same as on the previous occasions (none absenting themselves, for instance, to attend the races, for which he upbraided the congregation[s] in his sixth homily in the later Lent).

[2] Matt 5:45, rephrased to support the preacher's point. The Antiochene commentators set great store by this virtue of gentleness, πραότης, of which they often see David as an exemplar – as much out of character for him as it proved to be for a pastor like Chrysostom.

[3] Gen 2:19. Chrysostom is taking the account of life in the garden in a literalist way, and so is vulnerable to the criticism by non-believers that it does not square with the facts. At first he tries to contest that; then he admits it and explains on a moral basis the reversal of due order as due to sin. He likewise has no difficulty with a talking serpent.

[4] Just as the opening sermons have not explored the overall theological message of the composer of the creation story (of the universe) in Genesis 1, so differences in the second account in Genesis 2 (only in the homilies is this duplication acknowledged and defended – as a

didactic procedure of repetition by Moses) are not adverted to: we are still on the idea of government entrusted to human beings in 1:26, and a moral explanation of its subsequent curtailment, now presented as an example of divine solicitude.

[5] Gen 3:19. Chrysostom had above spoken of the Fall as a *felix culpa*, as the basis of our "rising" (resurrection in the full sense, or only from human weakness?); and here again he displays Eastern optimism by stressing the healing process rather than the sin. At this stage Adam is presented as primarily responsible for the Fall, a responsibility Chrysostom will later shift to his partner. (Modern readers would find the following comparison of the punitive master and divine compassion not to their taste; Chrysostom has no obvious difficulty with slavery.)

Sermon Four

[1] This time Chrysostom is definite that only one day had elapsed since the previous homily, and presumes that this congregation attended then as well. As he continues to be guided by the biblical text (1:26ff) in using ἄνθρωπος of the human being (not specifically the male for the time being), we may use the plural where it is not at variance with the text and where an English singular would be gender-specific.

[2] For an Antiochene a balance must be maintained in moral thinking between God's gift and human effort. Chrysostom here wants to insist that the high status of the human being was an instance of the former, but its loss lay in the area of the latter, where inadequacy manifests itself in ῥαθυμία, indifference, sloth, neglect – the

capital sin of our first parents, as he states also in the homilies ("original sin" not being a term found in his vocabulary).

3 Gen 2:18-20.

4 An Antiochene commentator finds value in precise details of the text, ἀκρίβεια being a virtue both of text and of commentator. If women had been among the congregation, one would like to think the preacher would have expatiated on the woman's greater virtues as a helpmate than the animals'.

5 Gen 3:16. Now the woman is the real culprit, and suffering for it by a condition of subjection. Would the prospect of a caring mate be solace enough?

6 Chrysostom sees the Genesis text and the Pastorals author reinforcing one another (a less happy example of the "harmony" of the Testaments) to disqualify women from any leadership or teaching function. Mlle Brottier benignly finds Chrysostom softening the full force of 1 Timothy 2:11-14; others may think he could hardly be more abrasive.

7 Found not in the Corinthian letters, in fact, but in Ephesians 5:25,33; Colossians 3:19.

8 Cf. Gen 9:20-25. Any women listeners (or subsequent readers) who had followed the argument so far would contrast the effort made to exonerate Eve and Noah, respectively. As usual, the reputation of patriarchal figures has to be protected.

9 Sir 3:10. The sages do not rate the title προφήτης.

10 Rom 13:3-4. We are at some distance from the Genesis text, though still generally on the effects of sin. As well as using conventional imagery to interest his congregation, Chrysostom can call on features of contemporary life, such as proper norms for imbibing, the ex-

ercise of punitive justice, strict mentors for children.

[11] Hab 1:13-14, the preacher (who cannot pause to check with a Bible, we have noticed) vaguely recalling this "minor" prophet (in Augustine's terminology).

[12] 1 Tim 1:9.

[13] Rom 13:1. The immediate distraction terminates Chrysostom's treatment of this point; when he recovers, he embarks on a different stage of the lecture.

[14] It may be that Chrysostom's departure from the text of Genesis to develop a rehearsed lecture on the various forms of government led to inattention on the part of the congregation, prompting him to break off and upbraid them in this beautiful aside which biographer Baur sees lending the sermon an "appearance of actuality." On the other hand, the aside is so stylized as also to suggest the possibility that Chrysostom had prepared for it, or that it was a later insertion, "appearance of actuality" being susceptible of manufacture in works in antiquity. Yet we still admire the preacher's sentiments and his esteem for his role in the ministry of the Word.

[15] Cf. Acts 20:7-9, a miracle story already embellished, and further developed by the preacher.

[16] Prov 27:6.

[17] Sir 3:7; 7:28.

[18] Exod 21:17; 20:12.

[19] Cf. Deut 21:18-21. We are even further from the text of Genesis as Chrysostom – even with relish – labors the point of lack of respect for parents and its punishment in OT times (omitting what von Rad sees as significant, the corroboration of the mother): was it a notorious abuse in his society? Perhaps Lenten sermons are the occasion to deal with it. He uses a term unknown to

the LXX, πατραλοία, for the guilty party, though parricide is hardly involved in the case he describes, nor in the Deuteronomy text.

[20] There is a suggestion here that the congregation became animated and expressed vocal support for the preacher's remarks on ungrateful children. In other cases he will acknowledge their applause (cf. Sermon Seven), positive responses which his rhetoric encourages – as likewise they could lose interest (this sermon betrays).

Sermon Five

[1] Chrysostom quite likely does detect the feeling in his congregation that they have bogged down and left the Genesis story behind. With typical ingenuity (and an implicit rebuke) he proffers a different image suggesting the need for further depth instead of forward progress; it is only laziness on their part, ῥᾳθυμία, he says.

[2] Today's women readers might not be so ready to concede that Eve alone was presented in a poor light in the previous homily.

[3] Though Chrysostom does not cite him here, this is Paul's argument in that key verse in Romans 5:12, "Death spread to all *inasmuch as* all have sinned," the conjunctive phrase ἐφ' ᾧ being taken thus by the Greek Fathers generally and most modern commentators. Women might still complain that the spotlight should not fall on them in particular.

[4] 1 Cor 7:13,16. Chrysostom is not likely to pursue the apparent contradiction between the previously cited Pastorals and 1 Corinthians on the basis of different

kinds of Pauline authorship.

[5] 1 Tim 2:12,14.

[6] Gen 3:16.

[7] 1 Cor 7:21-22. As noted before, Chrysostom does not think it opportune to contest the institution of slavery, even in his own society (Paul seeming to support him in this).

[8] Cf Dan 3:27. The three young men in the furnace are often cited by Chrysostom and other Antiochenes as examples of the righteous sufferer (as they appear also in paleo-Christian art, Irish high crosses, etc).

[9] Dan 3:14,16-17. Though we do not have a complete commentary on the book of Daniel from Chrysostom (as we do from Theodoret, who likewise takes it as ἱστορία), a reading of the text would have suggested to him that the three prisoners had spent many years at the court and by now would hardly have been callow youths.

[10] Cf. 2:27-28 in the version of Daniel by Theodotion (which the Antiochenes use in place of the LXX), where terms for astrologers and magicians are derived from places renowned for these arts, viz. Gezer and Chaldea.

[11] Dan 3:18.

[12] Job 1:9-10. As a good storyteller, Chrysostom realizes that the congregation may have enjoyed the sustained example of the young men but lost its connection with his theme (Genesis even further out of sight), so he proceeds to summarize.

[13] Cf. Dan 6:22.

[14] Acts 28:1-6. Though elsewhere Chrysostom will explain that βάρβαροι are more than merely non-Greek speakers (the classical sense), the term here (found in the text) may refer to the Maltese use of a form of the

Semitic Punic language, and thus incomprehensible.
[15] Luke 10:19; Rom 16:20; Gen 3:15 (the latter text – origi-
nally the focus of attention – now only marginal). Of the
three stages in our subjection to the effects of sin and
liberation from them, the practice of virtue precedes (typi-
cally for Antiochene morality) the assistance of Christ.
[16] Cf. Matt 25:34-36. With the systematic treatment of
sin and its effects over, the preacher turns to his equally
well-prepared parenesis on almsgiving that has eluded
him in his previous sermons.
[17] Chrysostom is a keen observer also of the plight of
the poor in his community, for whom there is clearly no
welfare system; almsgiving is their only source of assistance. Again, as in Sermon Four, with its mention of the
lamplighter, we gain the information that the
(para)liturgy was held late in the day.
[18] Cf. Luke 16:19-31. Unable to suggest some structured
approach in his society to endemic poverty, Chrysostom
can only invoke guilt and fear to prompt his congregation to occasional largesse. It is hardly a developed doctrine of social justice. Modern exegetes like J. Jeremias,
T. W. Manson and J. A. Fitzmyer likewise hold that Jesus'
words in the parable are not meant as "a comment on a
social problem," only as a reminder to people to examine their lives before it is too late.

Sermon Six

[1] Lent (an eight-week season in Chrysostom's church)
and especially its final forty days was a period when
(para)liturgies were held daily at which special sermons
were delivered to the congregation, "your good selves,"
ἡ ὑμετέρα ἀγάπη, a phrase akin to our "dearly beloved"

(cf. opening to Sermon Seven). Other clergy, "fathers," even the bishop, might also attend.

² We have noted that Chrysostom is a shrewd observer and commentator on social mores.

³ Matt 18:20. "Prophets and apostles" are present, for one thing, in the readings from Old and New Testaments, respectively. The list of topics covered (presumably in homilies) is also interesting. Chrysostom does not distinguish ways in which Jesus is present.

⁴ Did Chrysostom make such a promise? It does not appear in the sermons we have: has a sermon before this one been lost? On the other hand, a preacher could easily think he had formed such an intention when dealing with Genesis 2 in Sermon Three, just as much else of Chapters 2 and 3 was omitted as the preacher followed an agenda of his own.

⁵ Cf. Col 3:11.

⁶ Gen 2:19. As in his treatment of this verse in Sermon Three, there is not simply a literalism about Chrysostom's exegesis but also a naiveté.

⁷ Gen 2:23. Not having conducted a close commentary on the Genesis text, Chrysostom has not had much occasion to refer to alternative versions available to him in the Hexapla; here he cites the version found in Symmachus and Theodotion.

⁸ Gen 2:24. An Antiochene likes to highlight subtleties in the text in the interests of precision, ἀκρίβεια, a virtue for which he had just complimented the other translators. Chrysostom was unable to be precise enough to note the wordplay in the Hebrew in the previous verse between *ish/ishshah* reflected even in English man/woman but not in Greek.

⁹ Brottier informs us that Clement of Alexandria re-

ported gnostic views attributing to the serpent the gift of discernment to human beings. Chrysostom has devoted more attention to this issue of Adam's having a knowledge of right and wrong than, say, to a question of the equality of the sexes or marriage (cf. note 4 on Sermon Seven); it is germane to Antiochene morality, where human responsibility is a key factor.

[10] Chrysostom offers the vision of the Christian home as church in miniature, where the spiritual welfare of all members (servants included) is nourished in the manner of dining at table. The male householder, responsible for the welfare of all, promotes this in one form by reading "what has been said" (probably the Scriptures, as Chrysostom says elsewhere; hardly the preacher's text). It is a noble vision of the domestic church, especially by one who sets much store by what happens in his (para)liturgies.

[11] Matt 6:33.

Sermon Seven

[1] As we noted in connection with the rebuke delivered to the congregation in Sermon Four about their being distracted by the lamplighter, Chrysostom can also note their rapt attention or even applause. He takes this latter as confirmation of their accepting his advice to ruminate at home on "the words" – either his or the biblical authors' – and become an *ecclesiola*.

[2] Previous sermons in the series have been quite brief. The seventh is longer, perhaps suggesting that Chrysostom is the only speaker, with no bishop or other "fathers" present; and this may explain why he is taking some time to repeat a point made to the congrega-

tion at the close of the previous sermon, holding fast what they heard from the Scriptures ("the sayings," "God's word") and/or the preacher's "words." He proceeds to unfold the parable of the talents in support.

3 Cf. Matt 25:14-30, a parable that appeals to an Antiochene for its careful balance of divine gift and human effort, and its punishment of ῥᾳθυμία; Chrysostom comments on it frequently.

4 It was, in fact, just these topics in relation to Genesis 2:23-24 that (as we observed in note 9 to Sermon Six) Chrysostom excluded in favor of proving the human being's accountability. His approach to Genesis this Lent has been to seize upon items of the text that suit an agenda of his own.

5 Chrysostom has not, in fact, cited this verse Genesis 3:5 before; we noted how he declined to work systematically through the biblical text. Neither did he establish that the serpent of Genesis 3 is to be taken as the devil. Perhaps under the weight of tradition (visible also in his fellow Antiochenes), he bypasses the phenomenon of a talking snake to accept without question what the author did not intend. "The serpent which now enters the narrative," says von Rad, "is marked as one of God's created animals (2:19). In the narrator's mind it is scarcely an embodiment of a 'demonic' power and certainly not of Satan. What distinguishes it a little from the rest of the animals is exclusively its greater cleverness." Modern exegetes would fault Chrysostom for accepting without question the identification before putting to the text some such questions; his own agenda drives him on to some eisegesis.

6 Jn 8:44.

7 Cf. Mic 6:8; Jer 2:13. While it suits Chrysostom, in com-

ment on Genesis 3, to identify good and evil as obedience and disobedience respectively, it seems selective of him to choose a single passage from Jeremiah to establish the latter, and hardly true to the spirit of a celebrated locus in Micah to establish the former. Theodore of Mopsuestia, Chrysostom's fellow Antiochene (only fragments of his work on Genesis extant), expressed himself in similar terms.

[8] Gen 4:8,9. Chrysostom's rhetorical abilities would have made him a fearsome prosecutor. Again we have leapt to another incident in the primeval history to reinforce the point previously made in the series rather than allow the text itself to dictate progress, the downside being that key concerns of the author are passed over, such as the significance and aftermath of the Fall. Perhaps, with Genesis being regular Lenten fare, the preacher feels that this and other points have been made in previous years.

[9] Gen 4:12 LXX. Brottier excludes from her text the rest of the sentence.

[10] Cf. Gen 26:19-21; 21:31; 32:2. If, as Chrysostom claims, the point requires the support of many etiologies, they are forthcoming. But the reader feels that with this *makrologia*, for which he gained a bad name, members of the congregation could feel they were excused for going elsewhere (to the races, e.g., for which he vigorously upbraids them in Homily Six).

[11] Chrysostom, of course, is (mercifully) not in a position to discuss the threefold etiology in Penuel/Peniel found in Genesis 32:31-32. But he does counsel against taking the Jacob story in a way which infringes divine transcendence.

[12] Rom 5:20,15-16. Chrysostom has the support of Paul

– and indeed of all the East – in accentuating not so much the Fall and all lost in it as the benefits stemming from it, not so much the wound as the healing. While not overtly commenting on the text of Genesis 3, he is in touch with the New Testament's theological analysis of the episode (as Western Fathers tended not to be).

[13] Jn 1:29. Chrysostom again shows his concurrence with Paul's thought in Romans 5:12 in treating, not of the transmission of the sin ("fall," παράπτωμα) like Western Fathers, but of the participation of all by their own sins/falls. He continues to lend the "original sin" (not a term of his, of course) some proportion by putting it in context, insisting that human nature has not been impaired (as if again to contest Western positions).

[14] Luke 23:42. To strengthen his case (that this character was far worse than Adam) by stressing the lowly condition of the suppliant, Chrysostom chooses to describe him as a "brigand," λῃστής, which is however the term found in Matthew and Mark (where no such conversion is found), Luke using the less pejorative "criminal," κακοῦργος. At least Chrysostom has escaped the tendency to speak of "the good thief." His rhetorical skills would arouse any tiring listener.

[15] Matt 11:18; John 7.12. To make his case that, though sinning worse than Adam we can reach heaven by faith alone, Chrysostom is for the moment conveniently suppressing some key tenets of Antiochene morality.

[16] Luke 23:43.

[17] While patently subscribing to the odium in which the Manichees were held, Chrysostom shows some restraint in allowing their case against the resurrection of the body to be developed. We noted that in his selective treatment of Genesis 1-3 he had not highlighted one of

its key themes, the goodness of material things, which was anathema to these heretics, whereas dualism is not to Antioch's liking; so to a degree this digression is *ad rem*.

[18] Chrysostom is in no doubt of the divine inspiration of the Scriptures.

[19] 2 Cor 5:10; 1 Cor 15:53.

[20] 1 Cor 2:9; Matt 4:17. Chrysostom is contesting the Manichean denial of bodily resurrection, for which Jesus' promise of a welcome of the brigand into "paradise" that day was used in support. He wants to deny that heaven is referred to in the promise, using some biblical references to disqualify paradise on the reasoning that Adam's garden was not heaven, and that the brigand had not actually got to heaven and its "good things" so far, only paradise (a sort of halfway house – a notion he shared with Augustine). Modern exegetes also have a difficulty with "this day," E. E. Ellis concluding that the reference is to the day of messianic salvation inaugurated by the death of Jesus. G. B. Caird points out that the term paradise served to reflect a growing Jewish view of an afterlife (though not in the mind of the LXX when they adopted this Old Persian word for garden in Genesis 2 to render the Hebrew *gan*).

[21] Though the sermon has digressed onto the question of bodily resurrection, the underlying theme of what was lost and what was gained by the Fall surfaces, Eastern optimism prevailing.

[22] Jn 3:5.

[23] Jn 3:18; 5:24; Gen 2:17. All these citations are for Chrysostom cases of prolepsis (modern Johannine commentators would not agree), supporting his view that a person in paradise is *as good as* in heaven, like a mori-

bund person being as good as dead – a preferable interpretation to the Manichean one, in his view, not
"forced." (The LXX of Genesis 5:5 specifies nine hundred and thirty years as Adam's lifespan.)

[24] Heb 11:13,40. The brigand, like the patriarchs, had to
mark time. Has he been worth all the attention given
him – and largely off the point? (Interestingly, when
Chrysostom next day sums up this sermon in the presence of the bishop, he conveniently omits mention of
the brigand and all this digression.)

[25] Perhaps not all the congregation relish the prospect
of hearing more on this topic – whatever the day's topic
was meant to be, the direction having changed at times.
In some mss., including that followed in the PG edition, in place of the brief peroration appears the lengthy
one concluding Sermon Eight.

Sermon Eight

[1] Bishop Flavian and the local clergy are in attendance;
with conventional imagery Chrysostom acknowledges
their presence and promptly gets on with his job, time
being required later for perhaps another speaker.

[2] Gen 2:16. The summary of the previous day's sermon,
while helpful (especially for anyone not present then),
interestingly does not include mention of the brigand
on the cross and the lengthy digression on the Manichees
and debate as to whether admission to "paradise"
means getting into heaven. Why admit to the bishop
that you lost the plot?

[3] The figure of the Scriptures as divine communications
akin to imperial edicts occurs also in the larger series of

homilies. (The congregation is probably standing during the sermon.)

⁴ In beginning his *Quaestiones* on the Octateuch, Theodoret also recognized the need to confute those who maligned the Old Testament and its provisions, such as followers of Marcion.

⁵ Isa 8:20; Ps 119.105; Prov 6:23; Rom 2:17. Chrysostom is uncharacteristically obliged to cite flattering references to the (Mosaic) Law here in the process of justifying the law given in the garden – to which, of course, the authors cited were not referring.

⁶ Ps 147:12-14,19-20. Paradoxically, when Chrysostom about this time gives his lectures on the Psalter, he takes these "good things" in an anagogical sense, whereas here where it suits him to take references to the Law as meant for the law in the garden, he prefers a more literal interpretation.

⁷ Bar 3:10,12,22-23,29,35-36. This passage (which he cites also in his commentary on those verses in Psalm 147) in the deuterocanonical book of Baruch, attached in the LXX to Jeremiah, presents the "book of the commandments of God" (4:1) as Israel's exclusive possession of wisdom. Again Chrysostom would be aware that he is citing a further biblical encomium of the Mosaic Law to make his point about the law given to Adam in the garden (a scene now out of sight): why would he adopt this Jewish viewpoint – just to build a case (against the Marcionites) that any divine law is a blessing, not a curse? Is the presence of dignitaries affecting him?

⁸ Rom 3:1.

⁹ Chrysostom is aware that the biblical encomiums he cites refer to the Law "in writing;" surely he knows that the clergy present would realize he is drawing the long

bow. Or is the sermon not about the garden law but about Marcionites' and others' difficulty with divine law in general as a cause of sin?

[10] Heb 1:1-2; Rom 5:11; 1 Thess 4:16. For the moment Chrysostom switches focus to claim that Christians have a more direct relationship to the Lord – yet he at once returns to insisting that even in the beginning the Law was given personally (not the Mosaic Law now, given through Moses and/or an angel). As with some other of these sermons, the preacher has hardly been clear and consistent about the day's theme.

[11] As in the homilies, Chrysostom identifies ῥᾳθυμία as the capital sin. And, with typical Eastern optimism, he sees some other people, less indifferent, avoiding such a fall.

[12] Ps 119:103. This rather lengthy peroration (considering the complaint of lack of time) appears verbatim also in some mss. at the end of Sermon Seven. Chrysostom implies there will be further sermons in the series; if there were, we do not have them.

[13] Matt 25:35.

[14] Cf. 2 Cor 9:10. It has been a relatively brief sermon, perhaps allowing the bishop or another cleric to speak.

General Index

Index of biblical citations

Old Testament

Genesis
1-3, 7, 11
1:1, 15, 33, 34
1:26, 8, 9, 40, 43-49, 51,
    53-55, 62, 63
2:9, 97, 107, 114-20, 135
2:16-17, 132, 136, 167
2:18, 63-64
2:19-20, 56-57, 102
2:23, 102-104
3:5, 164
3:16, 10, 64-67, 135
3:19, 156
4:8-9, 165
4:12, 165
5:5, 168
9:20-25, 157
21:31, 165
26:19-21, 165
32:2, 165

Exodus
20:12, 158
21:17, 158

Deuteronomy
21:18-21, 12, 158

Job
1:9-10, 160

Psalms
33:9, 150
119:103, 170
119:105, 169
147:12-20, 169
148:1-2, 150

Proverbs
1:9, 149
6:23, 169
27:6, 158

Isaiah
1:16-18, 150
6:1-2, 153
8:20, 169
9:6, 153
43:26, 150
64:4, 152